Victoria and Albert Museum

Guide to English Embroidery

PATRICIA WARDLE

D1232819

London: Her Majesty's Stationery Office

ISBN 0 1 1 290030 5

The Victoria and Albert Museum has a particularly remarkable and complete collection of English Embroideries and a general guide to the subject has for long been in demand. This newly-written *Guide* gives a fuller account of the subject than its predecessor (*English Embroidery*, by Barbara Morris) and with over 90 illustrations covers more adequately the many varied aspects of the story. It begins with Anglo-Saxon times and goes down to the 1950s and the present day with (domestic) machine embroidery. "Opus Anglicanum", Elizabethan embroidery, the 17th and 18th centuries and the Victorian period are all dealt with. The social background and the demands of style and fashion, as they affected embroideries at different periods and in different degrees, are noted. The pieces illustrated are taken from the Museum's collections but are supplemented when necessary with important pieces elsewhere, such as the Bayeux Tapestry. Patricia Wardle worked for ten years in this Museum and for a large part of that time as Research Assistant in the Department of Textiles. She has published two books, *Victorian Silver* and *Victorian Lace,* and was responsible for the revised edition of A. F. Kendrick's *English Needlework.* Her successor in the Textile Department, Miss S. Levey, has collated the illustrations and bibliographical references and steered the book through the press.

GEORGE WINGFIELD DIGBY, *former Keeper, Department of Textiles*

English Embroidery

The history of English embroidery is long and complex. It includes within its scope the work of very different types of people: professional men or women supplying the exacting demands of court, church and aristocracy for sumptuous textiles, amateur needle-women using their skill to adorn themselves and their homes, little girls toiling through difficult tasks as part of their education. The embroideries that have survived to the present day, therefore, cover a wide range of uses and exhibit many levels of skill, while still in some measure reflecting the artistic fashions and social conditions of the period in which they were made.

Anglo-Saxon embroidery and the Bayeux Tapestry

The precise origins of English embroidery are unknown but the earliest surviving pieces show what a high degree of skill and sophistication its practitioners reached during the Anglo-Saxon period. The oldest English embroidery hitherto discovered in Western Europe is the so-called chasuble of SS. Harlindis and Relindis, preserved at Maeseyck in Belgium. That this embroidery in coloured silks and silver-gilt thread was originally a masterly piece of work is still apparent, although its present condition is a mere shadow of its original state. Its design of interlace and of birds and animals in medallions is comparable with Anglo-Saxon work in other media dating from the second half of the 9th century.[1]

The stole and maniple associated with St. Cuthbert (1) at Durham Cathedral are in a much better state of preservation and show clearly the fine technique of the Anglo-Saxon embroiderers, who must have been professionals. The hieratic style of these pieces, quite different from that of the Maeseyck chasuble, is related to contemporary continental art[2] and inscriptions on them show that they were made for Frithestan, Bishop of Winchester from 909 to 931, at the order of Queen Ælfflæd, who died in 916. It seems likely, indeed, that the work was done at Winchester, the Saxon capital.[3]

Written evidence indicates that embroideries were made at this time in quite a different style from these vestments:[4] hangings for secular or ecclesiastical use, for example, were sometimes adorned with the heroic deeds of a king or nobleman. Only one such piece has survived but it is, justly, one of the most famous of all embroideries, the Bayeux Tapestry (2). This embroidered hanging, over 230 feet long, is worked in coloured wools on a linen ground in a technique, laid and couched work combined with outline stitches, perfectly adapted to the rapid execution of a series of vivid scenes depicting the story of the

---

[1] M. Calberg, "Tissus et broderies attribués aux saintes Harlinde et Relinde" in *Bulletin de la Société Royale d'Archéologie de Bruxelles*, October 1951, pp. 1 ff.

[2] C. F. Battiscombe, *ed., The Relics of St. Cuthbert*, Oxford, 1956, p. 409.

[3] In the following century there occurs a reference in the will of Matilda, wife of William the Conqueror, to a chasuble embroidered by Alderet's wife at Winchester.

[4] References are given in Mrs. A. G. I. Christie, *English Medieval Embroidery*, Oxford, 1938, and A. F. Kendrick, *English Needlework*, 2nd ed., London, 1967.

Norman conquest of England. In style the Tapestry, like comparable contemporary manuscripts, still retains much of the liveliness characteristic of Anglo-Saxon art. It seems probable that it was commissioned by Odo, Bishop of Bayeux, for the adornment of his new cathedral, dedicated in 1077.[5]

Early medieval embroidery

The Normans seem to have appreciated and encouraged the work of the embroiderers among their new subjects. During the century and a half following the conquest it is possible to trace a steady development in both technique and artistic expression, a development that was to culminate in the flowering of *opus anglicanum*. Many of the embroideries of this period are worked in silver-gilt thread on grounds of dark-coloured silk. A fragment from the tomb of William of St. Carilef, Bishop of Durham 1081–96, shows how early the technique of underside-couching appeared.[6] This technique, in which silver-gilt threads laid on the surface of the silk were secured in a supple manner, being pulled through the ground material in small loops at regular intervals by means of linen threads carried over the back of the work, was used in many other parts of Europe, but it was brought to its greatest refinement and perfection in England. It appears on all the embroideries that survive from the 12th century, including pieces associated with St.

Thomas of Canterbury.[7] These are in a Romanesque style in which animals in medallions, leafy scrolls and stiffly drawn human figures predominate. It seems that by the end of the 12th century English embroidery was already known on the continent: an important example of this period is a cope preserved at Brunswick,[8] which is only one of a number of contemporary pieces in European collections.

During the first half of the 13th century the style of the embroideries gradually became less rigid, a development which may be traced in the dalmatic at Halberstadt Cathedral[9] and the vestments associated with St. Edmund Rich.[10] Fragments of a set of buskins and sandals from the tomb of Walter de Cantelupe, Bishop of Worcester 1236–66 (3), are decorated with figures of kings in leafy scrolls, foreshadowing the later Tree of Jesse design. The embroidery is executed in silver-gilt threads underside-couched in the simple brick pattern commonly used at this time.

Opus Anglicanum

The great period of *opus anglicanum* began in the middle of the 13th century, when its fame began to spread rapidly throughout Europe. The Clare Chasuble (4), dated by association with Margaret de Clare, wife of Edmund Plantagenet, Earl of Cornwall, to the years between her marriage in 1272 and divorce in 1294, shows the style current soon after the beginning of this, perhaps the finest period in all English embroidery.

[5] Sir F. Stenton, *ed., The Bayeux Tapestry*, London, 1957; C. R. Dodwell, "The Bayeux Tapestry and the French Secular Epic" in *Burlington Magazine*, Vol. CVIII, Nov. 1966, pp. 549–60.

[6] D. King, *Opus Anglicanum*, Victoria and Albert Museum and Arts Council Exhibition, London, 1963, No. 1.

[7] *Ibid.*, Nos. 2–4, 12. Christie, *op. cit.*, Nos. 11–13, 24.
[8] Christie, *op. cit.*, p. 72, Pls. XXV ff.

[9] *Ibid.*, p. 75, Pls. XXVIII, XXIX.
[10] *Ibid.*, Nos. 27–9; King, *op. cit.*, Nos. 19–22.

Here figures, in whose attenuated forms appear signs of a greater grace and vigour than had hitherto been customary, are arranged in quatrefoils surrounded by animals in leafy scrolls of much freer design than before. Here too may be seen the fine silk embroidery in split stitch which had been developed to delineate the most subtle *nuances* of feature and gesture. At about this time silver-gilt threads underside-couched in chevron pattern gradually replaced the older and more rigid brick pattern.

The high esteem in which English embroidery was held at this time is indicated by the Vatican Inventory of 1295, where there are listed more examples of *opus anglicanum* than of any other type of embroidery. The work was sought after by monarchs and church dignitaries all over the continent and many of the finest surviving pieces are still to be found in European churches and museums where they have long been treasured. *Opus anglicanum* was extremely costly and, apart from their artistic merits, the embroideries had a considerable intrinsic value thanks to the quantities of silver and silver-gilt thread, seed pearls and semi-precious stones that adorned them. There is evidence to show that the rich merchants of London considered the financing of such work to be a sound investment. Most of the embroidery was carried out in workshops in London by professional masters of the craft, some of whose names have been recorded. It is not possible now to identify the work of Rose de Burford who made a cope to the order of Edward II's queen in 1317, but many surviving pieces testify to the skill of such embroiderers, who had to serve a rigorous seven years' apprenticeship before they were considered qualified.

Around the turn of the century embroidery design began to reflect the lively naturalism of the contemporary decorated style in architecture. At first the decorative schemes of such vestments as copes, which called forth the highest talents of the em-broiderers, were still somewhat rigidly controlled: figures or scenes in shaped medallions arranged in rows being the favourite plan. Yet in a cope with the closely-related Tree of Jesse design (5) there appears a greater humanity and grace in the figures, while the vine leaves are rendered with a closely observed and delicate realism. The rose red silk of this cope was a favourite background material at this period.

A panel (6), probably from a cope, inscribed with the name of John of Thanet, a monk-musician of Canterbury cathedral, illustrates the greatest heights of majestic, hieratic design achieved by English embroiderers of the early 14th century, fully equalling any of the other artistic products of the time. The only other surviving piece bearing figures of such scale and dignity is the Melk chasuble[11] with its two Crucifixion scenes.

The Syon Cope (7), dating like these two pieces from about 1300–20, shows the continued popularity of the arrangement of scenes in linked compartments. The six-winged cherubim placed here between the compartments were a favourite motif in English embroidery throughout the Middle Ages. Typically English too is the way in which the participants in the various scenes are shown betraying their emotions through forceful gestures and striking facial expressions. Nothing is known about the designers of these embroideries but it seems fairly certain that they must have been closely connected with manuscript illuminators such as those of the contemporary East Anglian School, so great are the similarities in drawing between the two art forms. The Syon Cope, originally a bell-shaped chasuble, once belonged to a complete set of mass vestments of which other parts, embroidered with coats-of-arms, have been used to make the orphreys and morse. The cope is unusual at this period in that the linen ground is entirely covered with underside-couched red and green silk.

Backgrounds of silver-gilt embroidery were much

[11] King, *op. cit.*, No. 39; Christie, *op. cit.*, No. 68.

more common now and were executed with the most consummate skill. On a panel from a burse of about 1310–40 (8) and on the Marnhull orphrey (9) scenes rendered with the utmost delicacy and refinement are set off by shimmering grounds worked with elaborate heraldic devices which are most cunningly managed so as to enhance rather than compete with the all-important subject-matter. These pieces are close in style to many of the finest surviving examples of *opus anglicanum*, such as the copes at Pienza,[12] Bologna,[13] and Toledo,[14] and the Tree of Jesse orphrey at Lyon.[15] In all of them may be seen decorative details such as angels, heads of prophets and apostles, birds and foliage, blending with the pictorial subject-matter but never obscuring it.

In the second quarter of the 14th century plain velvet grounds came into use, the embroidery being worked on them through a piece of thin cloth on which the design was drawn and which was laid on the pile surface to facilitate the stitchery. Now the figures become noticeably more elegant and the emphasis is on charm rather than on depth of religious feeling. The Butler-Bowdon Cope (10) has figures and scenes under concentric rows of arcading, an arrangement which had by this time become the most usual form of cope design. Each of the three main subjects occupying the centre back of the cope, i.e. the most important position in the design, expresses a devotion to the Virgin Mary highly characteristic of the period. Delightful scenes of the early life of the Virgin and the nativity of Christ appear on a set of red velvet alb-apparels of similar date (12), which bear the arms of Bardolf and another English family.

Very few secular embroideries have survived from the Middle Ages, although many descriptions are known of hangings and costumes adorned with fanciful or heraldic devices. Such fragments as remain show that applied work and woollen embroidery[16] were used as well as richer techniques comparable to those familiar from ecclesiastical work.[17] The finest surviving secular embroidery, dating from the second quarter of the 14th century, is worked with the heraldic leopards of England in silver-gilt thread on a red velvet ground.[18] It probably once formed part of a horse-trapper and owes its preservation to having been made into a chasuble.

Medieval amateur work is even rarer, only one example being so far known: an altar-frontlet of the early 14th century bearing the name of Domina Johanna Beverley, the nun who made it.[19] It is completely different both in style and technique from contemporary professional work.

About the middle of the 14th century a more severe style, related to perpendicular architecture, began to appear in embroidery. Elaborately ornamented silver-gilt grounds were now replaced by grounds worked in lattice designs and figures were more rigidly drawn. A cope orphrey of the third quarter of the century (11) illustrates this style. It also shows a new departure in technique, inasmuch as the noses of the figures and the lines of their drapery are raised and padded. This feature appears on other contemporary embroideries, notably the cope at Vich[20] in Spain, the last of the great English copes.

[12] King, *op. cit.*, No. 54; Christie, *op. cit.*, No. 95.
[13] King, *op. cit.*, No. 53. Christie, *op. cit.*, No. 86.

[14] Christie, *op. cit.*, p. 156, Pl. cix.
[15] King, *op. cit.*, No. 57; Christie, *op. cit.*, No. 61.

[16] King, *op. cit.*, Nos. 29, 31.
[17] *Ibid.*, Nos. 44, 74.
[18] *Ibid.*, No. 76.

[19] This piece is in the Victoria and Albert Museum (T.70–1923). See King, *op. cit.*, No. 43.

[20] *Ibid.*, No. 91; Christie, *op. cit.*, No. 89.

Embroidery from the end of the 14th century to the Reformation

Opus anglicanum had by now passed its peak and the Black Death and the wars of the end of the 14th century finally put an end to this great period of English embroidery. Large quantities of ecclesiastical embroidery continued to be produced and much of it found a ready market abroad, but it was now inferior in both design and technique to previous work and English design, instead of standing pre-eminent, began to follow fashions current elsewhere in Europe. An orphrey of the end of the 14th or beginning of the 15th century (13) illustrates the soft figure style and imprecise drawing of this period, as well as showing a typical architectural setting and a silver-gilt background worked partly over thick linen threads to give a raised appearance. The effect produced by this technique is generally rather crude in comparison with the refinements of underside-couching, which was rapidly going out of use.

Richly patterned Italian silk brocades and velvets were now used for vestments and embroidery played a lesser role in the finished result, being restricted to orphreys separately embroidered on linen, and no longer covering the whole garment. Even the designs of orphreys became more and more stereotyped, no doubt to allow for greater speed and ease of production. Scenes in the life of the Virgin, pairs of saints under architectural canopies or representations of the Crucifixion were now standard subjects. A typical Crucifixion scene appears on a chasuble of Italian velvet and cloth-of-gold, which is dated by a coat-of-arms of Henry de Beauchamp, Duke of Warwick, to the years between his marriage to Lady Cecily Neville in 1434 and his death in 1445 (14).

The Virgin and Child on the hood of the Walston Cope (15) exemplify a new figure style, notable for heavy, massed draperies, which came into England in the second half of the 15th century from Flanders, the country which had now taken the lead in Western European embroidery.

During the 15th century the practice grew up of embroidering motifs separately, cutting them out and applying them to a silk or velvet ground, a comparatively quick way of producing a richly decorated textile. The effect was usually enhanced by couched silver-gilt threads worked on the ground material around the motifs. Many vestments and altar-hangings of this type have survived. They usually bear a central motif, such as the Annunciation or the Assumption of the Virgin (16), surrounded by lilies, bells, winged cherubs on wheels or similar motifs. At this time too it became quite common for embroideries to bear either the rebus or the arms of the donor or even embroidered portraits of the persons in question, often combined with requests for prayers (17, 18). Perhaps this may be taken as an indication of the increasing importance of the individual and of secular considerations in contemporary life and of the rise of a new type of society. In this connection it is significant that the finest surviving embroideries of the period immediately preceding the Reformation are the great funeral palls commissioned by the rich merchants of the City of London.[21]

With the Reformation the great tradition of ecclesiastical embroidery in England came to an end. A few pieces may date from somewhat later in the 16th century but these are in general of minor significance. A chalice veil (19), for example, soberly adorned with a verse from a metrical translation of Psalm 51, is an indication of the religious outlook of post-Reformation England. It may also serve as a reminder

[21] King, *op. cit.*, Nos. 149–154; Victoria and Albert Museum, *An Exhibition of Works of Art belonging to the livery companies of the City of London*, 1926. 2nd ed., 1927.

of lighter varieties of ecclesiastical embroidery,[22] most examples of which have long since perished, although they are often recorded in inventories.

Early 16th century secular embroidery

The advent of the Tudor monarchy brought to England a return of settled conditions and an increase in prosperity. Now the aristocracy and the wealthier members of the new middle class began to direct more of their attention to the decoration of their houses as well as their persons. Inventories such as those of Dame Agnes Hungerford in 1523[23] and Katharine of Aragon in 1536[24] are full of references to hangings and cushions of rich silks or velvets embroidered, often in silver-gilt thread, with formal arabesque ornament, with heraldic devices or with floral designs. Surviving embroideries of this period are rare, but a bed-hanging[25] with the arms of the Wentworth family (20), which dates from about 1554, may be taken as a characteristic example of the popular "paned" or "paled" work of the period. It is made of crimson silk and ivory damask embellished with silk cord couched in a design of formal quatrefoils enclosing flower motifs which foreshadow those familiar in Elizabethan embroidery.

Meticulous work of this nature must have been executed by professionals, but the amateur embroideress was at last beginning to come into her own. Among Dame Agnes Hungerford's possessions, for example, was a casket containing various types of silver-gilt thread, including "Venyse golde" and "damaske golde", and coloured silks for embroidery, while surviving embroideries by Queen Katharine Parr and the young Princess Elizabeth[26] show that the most noble ladies did not disdain this occupation.

Elizabethan embroidery

In the Elizabethan period the new tradition of domestic embroidery came to full flower and now for the first time the work of amateurs assumed an equal importance with that of professionals. Indeed, it is often impossible to distinguish between them. Much of the most elaborate professional work, such as formal court costume lavishly embroidered with metal thread and jewels, costumes for masques and heraldic embroidery, has now vanished completely, but it is clear that professionals also produced pieces in the simpler styles and techniques favoured by amateur needlewomen. Some surviving pieces, such as bookcovers or richly embroidered gloves like those given by Queen Elizabeth to Margaret Edgecumbe (37), are obviously professional work; others, such as a red satin cushion adorned with perfectly drawn flower sprigs within a formal arrangement of coiling stems (25), are so finely and precisely executed as to suggest the hand of a professional. But amateur work was often of a high standard too, though an amateur may sometimes betray herself by embellishing

---

[22] A rare 16th century pyx-veil in white linen openwork is described in King, *op. cit.*, No. 165.

[23] *Archaeologia*, Vol. XXXVIII, 1860, p. 363.
[24] *Camden Miscellany*, Vol. III, 1854, pp. 23 ff.

[25] This panel was meant to be hung at the head of the bed. A matching panel, now in Ipswich Museum, was perhaps intended for the foot.

[26] C. Davenport, *English Embroidered Bookbindings*, London, 1899, pp. 32-36.

her work with her name in large letters (39) in contrast to the anonymity of the professional. Often a noble household would include a professional embroiderer to direct the work, even though the bulk of it might be done by the mistress of the house with the aid of her maids or even of the grooms and boys of the household, whom Bess of Hardwick is known to have pressed into the service of the needle.[27] This new emphasis on amateur and domestic embroidery gave rise to new techniques adapted to execution by non-professionals, quite different in character from the refined skills of *opus anglicanum*.

Embroidery on linen canvas in tent or varieties of cross stitch now came into prominence for the first time, destined to remain a favourite technique for the amateur to the present day. It was used for hangings, bed-valances (27), table and cupboard carpets (21, 22) and for the cushions (23, 39), often rectangular in shape, which were used to make benches and window seats more comfortable. This technique was also popular for applied work, an embroidery tradition carried over from the later Middle Ages. After the Reformation, indeed, many ecclesiastical pieces had been converted to secular use and embroidered motifs were often cut out and re-applied. Applied work had a special appeal for amateurs since it was much easier to decorate a silk or velvet hanging or cushion with small motifs worked separately on linen and afterwards applied than to attempt to embroider directly on to the richer material itself. Many linen panels worked with motifs for applied work have survived, and the way in which such motifs were used is illustrated here by

a fine long cushion cover of black velvet (24). This still retains the silk damask lining and the silk and silver-gilt fringe and tassels with which such cushions were normally trimmed. More sophisticated types of applied work in rich materials[28] or in woollen cloth (26) were also popular.

The subject matter of these furnishing embroideries often reflects the literary taste of the Elizabethans as well as their delight in flowers, gardens and the countryside. Patterns of a formal type such as the interlace in the Gifford table carpet (21) are fairly common, but it is usual for them to be combined with some of the favourite floral motifs of the period, perhaps a wreath of flowers as on the Gifford carpet, or sprigs placed between formal ornament,[29] or an exuberant vine twined round a trellis as on the Bradford table carpet (22). Boldly drawn flowers, often with attendant insects, appear on many embroideries (23, 24), whilst more formal arrangements of flowers, fruit and strapwork often form the borders of pictorial pieces.[30] In pictorial subjects gardens and the countryside play an important part. Typical country scenes with shepherds, hunting scenes, anglers and a noble pair strolling in front of their country house occur in the border of the Bradford table carpet. Other favourite subjects, such as the Old Testament stories or the tales from Ovid's *Metamorphoses* so often found on bed-valances, were usually placed in a country setting or in an elaborate formal garden with flowerbeds, fountain and arbour. A distinct group of such valances (27) bears figures clad in elaborate court costume of French type and it is thought that this style may have been introduced by Mary Queen of

[27] G. F. Wingfield Digby, *Elizabethan Embroidery*, London, 1963, p. 62.
[28] *Ibid.*, Pls. 58 and 68.

[29] Cf. another table carpet in the Museum (T.41–1928); J. L. Nevinson, *Catalogue of English Domestic Embroidery of the 16th and 17th centuries*, 2nd

ed., London, 1950, p. 8 and Pl. IV.

[30] Cf. the coverlet or hanging (T.125–1913) and accompanying bed-valances (T.129–134–1913); Nevinson, *op. cit.*, pp. 34–6 and Pls. XXV, XXVI.

Scots, particularly as many of the pieces have Scottish provenances.[31]

Mary Queen of Scots was herself an accomplished needlewoman and the stories of how she solaced her imprisonment with embroidery and tried to soften her captors with gifts worked by her own hand are well known.[32] The set of hangings, one of which is dated 1570, which Mary and Bess of Hardwick made together,[33] epitomize many of the aspects of Elizabethan amateur embroidery. To a ground of green velvet decorated with a formal design in couched cord are applied panels worked on linen canvas (28). Some of these panels bear the monograms of the two ladies, while the central panel on each hanging bears a device referring to the circumstances of their lives by means of the emblems so dear to the Elizabethans. The Queen of Scots copied some of the emblems on the panel shown here from one of the best-known compilations of the time, *Devises Heroïques* by Claude Paradin, published at Lyon in 1557. Other panels are worked with animals, birds, fish and fabulous creatures, most of them adapted from Conrad Gesner's *Icones Animalium*, 2nd edition, published at Zurich in 1560, while yet others bear flower sprigs. The sources of these particular flowers have not been traced, but the Elizabethan embroideress had at her disposal many contemporary herbals as well as the occasional book published specially for embroidery, such as Jacques Le Moyne De Morgue's *La Clef des Champs*, published in London in 1586.

Favourite flowers such as the rose, viola, honeysuckle and daffodil, arranged within interlacing patterns or on coiling stems, were particularly popular for the fine linen embroidery used for long pillow covers (30, 31[34]), for cupboard cloths and light covers, and for informal costume such as jackets (32), shirts, shifts, handkerchiefs, coifs (35) and forehead cloths, hoods (34) and men's caps (33). The techniques developed for this linen embroidery show the delight the Elizabethan needlewoman took in fine stitchery for its own sake. They included whitework (35), which was common to most Western European countries at this period and which was closely related to the fine *reticella* needlepoint lace favoured for collars, cuffs and other trimmings.

A technique that seems to have developed in a specifically English way was blackwork (29, 30, 34). This had its origin in the linear monochrome embroidery worked in double-running or Holbein stitch which was popular all over Europe in the earlier part of the 16th century. In Elizabethan blackwork a greater variety of stitch is usually to be found, with much emphasis on the use of geometric or floral filling patterns to give richness to a design (30). Perhaps part of the popularity of blackwork may be attributed to the ease with which it lent itself to the copying of printed illustrations in books. The cover known as "The Shepheard Buss" (29), for example, includes precise renderings of devices from Paradin, while on the hood with the coiling stem design (34) can be seen shading in minute stitches which is reminiscent of printing effects. Monochrome embroideries were worked in other colours, too, but black seems to have been the most popular.

Blackwork was often heightened in effect by the use of silver and silver-gilt thread, and such metal

[31] Wingfield Digby, *op. cit.*, pp. 134–36.

[32] Wingfield Digby, *op. cit.*, ch. 6.

[33] F. de Zulueta, *Embroideries of Mary Stuart and Elizabeth Talbot at Oxburgh Hall, Norfolk*, Oxford, 1923.

[34] This pillowcase comes from a set of which other examples are to be found in the Richmond and Untermeyer Collections.

threads figured prominently in other varieties of linen embroidery. Designs of great brilliance and gaiety were created in which stems were worked in plaited or chained stitches in silver or silver-gilt and flowers in detached buttonhole stitch in bright colours (31). Sometimes pieces were executed entirely in metal threads and spangles (33), while even richer techniques were used for small objects such as purses (36). These often bore designs of flowers in which the petals were raised by padding or by being worked separately and only partly attached to the linen canvas ground, which was frequently entirely covered with metal thread embroidery.

The motifs used on these little purses are sometimes found, in combination with flowers, birds and animals in tent stitch, on samplers of the so-called "spot motif" type,[35] These samplers, the majority of which seem to be of early or mid-17th century date, appear to be collections of patterns assembled with a view to future use. The earliest dated English sampler so far known, though quite different in style (38), also seems to be a compilation of designs.[36] It was made by Jane Bostocke in 1598, perhaps as a present for the little girl whose birth in 1596 is recorded in stitchery. Samplers are frequently referred to in Elizabethan and, indeed, in earlier writings,[37] but few surviving examples can be attributed to this period. Amongst their number are a few canvas trial pieces worked with designs suitable for table carpets or long cushions,[38] and perhaps some of the many surviving long, narrow linen samplers,[39] worked with rows of designs in whitework, cutwork and coloured silk embroidery. The latter seem almost

from their inception to have been technical exercises rather than collections of patterns for practical use.

17th century

The Elizabethan tradition of embroidery continued to flourish during at least the first quarter of the 17th century. In canvas work fewer large pieces are found and floral designs tended to become bolder with exotic blooms coming in to join the familiar favourites. Typical examples may be seen on a long cushion cover bearing the proud signature of its amateur worker and the arms of James I (39), together with animals of the type so frequently encountered in later 17th century embroidery. A pictorial canvas work design of the period is a cover for a Bible, dated 1613, with the Sacrifice of Isaac on one side and Jonah and the Whale on the other (41).

A new departure of the second quarter of the century was a short-lived revival of ecclesiastical embroidery, under the *aegis* of Archbishop Laud, who tried to reintroduce richness and splendour into church decoration and ritual in reaction against the austerity of Elizabethan days. A chalice veil (42), embroidered in red with the Symbols of the Passion and cherubs' heads, is a characteristic example of the design of this period. It was probably made by an amateur needlewoman, but many of the rich metal-thread embroidered church furnishings recorded in contemporary inventories must have been the work

---

[35] King, *Samplers*, 1960, pp. 5–6.

[36] King, "The Earliest Dated Sampler" in *Connoisseur*, Vol. CXLIX, 1962, p. 234.

[37] King, *Samplers*, pp. 2–3

[38] *Ibid.*, p. 4, note 5.
[39] *Ibid.*, pp. 5–6.

of professionals, to judge from a superb hanging of 1633 in the Museum's collection.[40]

Perhaps this piece may even have been the work of the most famous professional embroiderer of the day, Edmund Harrison, principal embroiderer to Charles I and later to Charles II.[41] Most of Harrison's work, heraldic embroidery, embroidered court costume and costumes for masques and plays,[42] has disappeared but, by good fortune, a set of pictures has survived (43).[43] The pictures, dated 1637, represent scenes in the life of the Virgin and the infancy of Christ. They are worked mainly in couched silver-gilt thread by the *or nué* method developed in Flanders, a fact which may indicate that Harrison received his training abroad.

Pictorial embroidery, used for practical purposes in Elizabethan times, began in the 17th century to be admired for its own sake. Some surviving pieces, such as the canvas work panel with the story of Abraham and the Angels (47), were no doubt originally made up as cushions in continuation of the Elizabethan tradition, but the vast majority were intended simply for framing as pictures. The earliest examples seem to have been small square tent stitch pictures, usually meticulously drawn and worked in minute stitches,[44] but it was not long before similar pictures began to be executed in flat silk stitchery[45] or in the three-dimensional technique known as stumpwork[46] on grounds of ivory-coloured satin. Stumpwork seems to have become popular about 1650 and to have

died out during the 1680s.[47] It most probably developed out of the three-dimensional effects already in use in Elizabethan embroidery, i.e. raised metal thread embroidery, padding or details worked in detached buttonhole stitch and only partly attached to the ground. All these devices were carried over to and elaborated in stumpwork, which also featured darned silk pile, metal strip, and the use of small wooden or ivory faces and hands for figures. The persistence of Elizabethan traditions is clearly evident too in the subject-matter of these pictures, even though the figures now often appear in 17th century costume. Old Testament subjects and stories from Ovid remained firm favourites and Bathsheba, for example, may frequently be seen bathing under an arbour or by a fountain, while David looks on from a curtained pavilion, in a country landscape with fantastic castles, all these scenic devices being borrowed from the pictorial valances of the previous century. Other popular subjects were figures personifying the Seasons, the Five Senses, or the Elements, representations of kings and queens and portrait busts in oval medallions.[48] Each figure or scene in the picture was usually perched on its own little piece of grass, the spaces between were filled up with disproportionately large flowers and insects, or with animals such as the lion, leopard, unicorn or stag, while clouds, the sun and the moon often completed the top of the picture.

Pictorial embroidery in tent stitch, flat silk stitchery

[40] T.108–1963, see P. Wardle, "A Laudian Embroidery" in *Victoria and Albert Museum Bulletin*, Vol. 1, 1965, pp. 24–8.

[41] C. Holford, *A Chat about the Broderers' Company*, London, 1910, pp. xiii and 151–53.
[42] *Walpole Society*, Vol. XII, 1923–24, p. 17.
[43] Kendrick, *English Needlework*, 1967, pp. 110–12.

[44] Wardle, "English Pictorial Embroidery of the 17th century" in *Antiques International*, London, 1966, p. 278, Fig. 4.
[45] An unfinished example (T.93–1964) in the Museum is dated 1636.

[46] The earliest use of the term seems to be a reference to "embroidery on the stamp" in *A New and Complete Dictionary of Arts and Sciences*, published in London in 1754–55.
[47] A late picture in the Museum is dated 1686 (T.17–1946).

[48] In a quite different category and undoubtedly professional work are the embroidered oval medallion portraits of Charles I, see Nevinson, "The Embroidered Miniature Portraits of Charles I" in *Apollo*, Vol. LXXXII, 1965, p. 310.

or stumpwork was also used to cover small books, mirror-frames, boxes and small cabinets. Boxes and cabinets often bore scenes depicting episodes in a single story such as that of Abraham or Joseph. They were used for trinkets and were generally finished off with a lining of silk, a mirror or print on the inside of the lid, and embroidery of geometric flowers in laid work on the internal drawers and doors. Sometimes a box would be entirely covered with laid work,[49] or it might have a very elaborate three-dimensional garden inside the lid.[50]

The designs were adapted to the purpose for which the embroidery was intended but, nonetheless, in pictures or objects of all techniques the same elements are repeated so often as to suggest the existence of a central source or sources from which designs might be obtained drawn out ready for working. Many of the figure subjects, like those of the previous century, were adapted from engravings such as those of Crispin de Passe[51] or in Gerard de Jode's *Thesaurus Sacrarum Historiarum Veteris Testamenti*, published in 1585.[52] Flowers and similar motifs were adapted from examples in publications such as those of Peter Stent and John Overton in the 1660s and 1670s.[53] Nonetheless the compositions are naïve and betray a childish taste. There exists, in fact, plenty of evidence both in documents[54] and on the embroideries themselves to show that they were mostly the work of little girls, who often reached a high level of technical accomplishment at an early age.[55]

The surviving work of Martha Edlin gives a clear picture of the rigorous training in embroidery undergone by girls in the 17th century. Martha completed her coloured sampler in 1668 at the age of eight, and her whitework one in the following year. These samplers, typical of the period, are worked in various techniques, including cutwork, with designs derived ultimately from 16th century pattern books and perpetuated in such publications as *The Needle's Excellency*, published by James Boler (10th edition, 1634). By the 1660s such samplers bore little or no relation to the varieties of embroidery in current practical use and their only purpose was to serve as a technical exercise. This, indeed, applied to most of this childish embroidery. Martha next tackled her cabinet, which featured the Seven Virtues, Music and the Four Elements and was finished in 1671. It still contains sundry pincushions and other small items worked by her as well as a set of silver toys perhaps given her as a reward for her industry. Her final piece of work was a beadwork jewel box, finished in 1673 (48). In this the beads are sewn to a satin ground, but beadwork on canvas or wire was also popular,[56] the most spectacular surviving objects being baskets bedecked with elaborate three-dimensional flowers.

Pictorial embroidery was not the only part of the Elizabethan tradition to suffer a sea-change in the 17th century. For the first quarter of the century linen embroidery remained much the same. Covers, pillow-covers, coifs, jackets and caps were still adorned with

---

[49] Cf. T.31–1935, dated 1683.
[50] Cf. T.23–1928. Nevinson, *Catalogue of English Domestic Embroidery*, 1950, pp. 52–3, and Pl. XXXVI.

[51] Nevinson, "English Domestic Embroidery Patterns of the 16th and 17th centuries" in *Walpole Society*, Vol. XXVIII, 1939–40, Pl. V.
[52] N. G. Cabot, "Pattern Sources of Scriptural Subjects in Tudor and Stuart Embroideries" in *Bulletin of the*

Needle and Bobbin Club, New York, Vol. XXX, 1946, p. 33.
[53] Nevinson, "Peter Stent and John Overton, Publishers of Embroidery Designs" in *Apollo*, Vol. XXI, 1936, p. 279.

[54] Kendrick, *English Needlework*, 1967, pp. 129–30.
[55] A good example in the Museum is a picture (T.48–1954) signed by Martha Hollis, aged 10, and dated 1660; see *Antiques International*, 1966, Pl. facing p. 285.

[56] Cf. T.69–1936 and T.72 and A–1926, Nevinson, *Catalogue of English Domestic Embroidery*, 1950, p. 57 and Pls. XL and LXXII.

coiling stems or delicate floral sprigs, although some of the designs of this period show a greater boldness and freedom.[57] A set of pillow-covers worked with stories from Genesis (40) illustrates the occasional use of pictorial themes in linen embroidery. Monochrome work remained popular. A shirt of this period (44) is embroidered in pink silk with typical motifs, some of them copied from a contemporary pattern book, Richard Shorleyker's *A Schole-House for the Needle*, published in 1624. The latest known reference to blackwork is dated 1633,[58] but this by no means represents the end of this tradition of embroidery.

Some hint of the new direction it was to take is to be found in Shorleyker's introduction to his book in which he mentions "sundry sorts of spots, as Flowers, Birds and Fishes, etc. . . . to be wrought, some with Gould, some with Silke, and some with Crewell, or otherwise at your pleasure." On a woman's jacket of the 1630s (45) may be seen motifs of this type worked in various outline stitches and shaded with speckling in precisely the same manner as contemporary blackwork, but now in red crewel wool[59] on a ground of cotton and linen twill weave.

This new material was far stronger than the linen previously used and its potentialities were soon appreciated and exploited. By the middle of the century crewelwork was being used for bedhangings in preference to canvas work or applied work. The old tradition of design lingered on, however. A cur- tain of mid-17th century date[60] (46) is still patterned with coiling stems bearing violas and honeysuckle alongside more exotic blooms. In the second half of the century such designs were rapidly superseded by much bolder arrangements of curving branches or trees bearing elaborate baroque leaves similar to those to be found on Flemish verdure tapestries or, on a much smaller scale, in Venetian needlepoint lace. They were often still worked in monochrome as well as in sombre browns and greens. Sprigs of naturalistic flowers, oak and ivy appear among the leaves and the elaborate filling devices used to enhance the design are an enlarged and adapted version of those familiar in blackwork. Some of the crewelwork designs of this period are naïvely drawn and are clearly the work of amateurs such as Abigail Pett, who included a fishpond and animals borrowed from contemporary stumpwork in the design of her bedhangings.[61] In general, however, the designs are much more accom- plished, indicating the hand of the professional in the drawing if not always in the stitchery. Patterns of this type were sent out to India to be copied and the resulting interplay of influences from India, China and Europe[62] had a noticeable effect on crewelwork design by the end of the century. Touches of brighter colour and exotic birds and animals can be seen amongst the heavy leaves on a hanging from a set dated 1696 (55).[63]

Further evidence of the part that oriental influence

[57] Cf. T.280–1927 and T.173–1931, Nevinson, *op. cit.*, pp. 19–20 and Pls. XVI and XVII.
[58] In the Howard of Na- worth Accounts, *Surtees Society*, 1878, p. 297.

[59] The word crewel means a thin worsted yarn composed of two strands.
[60] Other curtains from this set of four are in the Depart- ment of Circulation, Victoria and Albert Museum, the Royal Scottish Museum and Lady Richmond's Collection.

[61] T.13 to I–1929. Nevinson, *Catalogue of English Domestic Embroidery*, 1950, p. 61 and Pl. XLIII.
[62] J. Irwin, "Origins of the 'Oriental Style' in English Decorative Art" in *Burlington Magazine*, Vol. XCVII, 1955, pp. 106–14.

[63] The dated curtain from this set is in the Royal On- tario Museum, Toronto; K. B. Brett, "English Crewelwork Curtains in the Royal Ontario Museum" in *Embroidery*, Spring, 1965, pp. 13–15.

was beginning to play in English embroidery design by the end of the 17th century is provided by a coverlet worked in 1694 by Sarah Thurstone (57)[64] with small scenes in the Chinese manner featuring trees, rocks, pavilions, pagodas and bridges in brightly coloured silks.

For the most part, however, embroideries of the latter part of the 17th century are designed in the contemporary European mode. A set of hangings from Hatton Garden (53), executed in a wide range of stitches on a canvas ground, bear the elaborate leaves and flowers of crewelwork entwined round classical arcading, as well as favourite animals of the period. Although canvas work, usually in floral designs, was sometimes used for upholstery (50) in the middle years of the century after long cushions went out of fashion, it was not until the last quarter that it began to become really popular for this purpose. A typical example of this later period is a chair covered with a bold design of flowers and leaves (49). Small boxes continued to be covered with canvas work to the end of the century; another of the period's favourite floral designs may be seen on a box dated 1692 (51), executed in rococo stitch by Parnell Mackett, whose initials it bears.

A technique which enjoyed a great vogue in the late 17th and early 18th century was knotting. Ladies delighted in occupying their hands by making series of knots in linen threads of various thicknesses by means of a shuttle; Sedley's epigram reports that Queen Mary II, "when she rides in coach abroad, Is always knotting threads." The finished knotting was couched down to a ground material in designs often of considerable complexity. On a set of chairs of the early 18th century at Ham House (52) red knotting has been used to create a controlled design of strapwork, foliage, scrolls and flowers on a yellow silk ground.

Similar rather formal designs in couched cord or

metal thread were used to decorate hangings and costume. A bed of about 1690, for example, which belonged to one of William III's ministers, is covered with silk damask adorned with red braid in a design showing strong French influence (54). Such formal patterns are in marked contrast to the designs of contemporary crewel and canvas work.

18th century

While many techniques and designs popular in the late 17th century were carried over into the 18th, the early part of the new century witnessed a considerable revival of embroidery for practical purposes. No longer are the majority of surviving pieces the work of children, although little girls still continued to work samplers as part of their schooling. These, however, gradually ceased to be such formidable technical exercises as the long narrow sampler was superseded by a squarer variety[65] worked on a woollen canvas ground with rows of letters, figures, formal motifs and verses in cross or eyelet stitches, perhaps enlivened by a figure or a border of flowers in long and short and stem stitches, or a small panel of Florentine or rococo stitch. Embroidered pictures in canvas work or flat silk embroidery continued to enjoy a certain vogue, portraits of royalty or contemporary celebrities, pastoral scenes and country houses (65) being favourite subjects, but, generally speaking, at this period, as in Elizabethan times, pictorial designs were worked on objects meant for practical use.

They were especially common on canvas work, one of the most popular techniques of the period. Typical examples are a set of chair seats (63) and cushion covers adorned with hunting scenes within borders

[64] A similar coverlet worked by Mary Thurstone is in the Fitzwilliam Museum, Cambridge; see *Connoisseur*, LXXXII, 1928, pp. 94–9.
[65] King, *Samplers*, pp. 8–9.

of bold flowers. Classical,[66] theatrical and pastoral scenes were also favoured for the upholstery of chairs and settees as well as for screens of all types (66) and for card-table tops. The contemporary delight in Chinoiserie is illustrated here by one of a pair of canvas work screen panels (58) with pictorial subjects. Chinese birds, flowers and blue and white vases are often to be found on canvas work too.

But, whatever the subject-matter, the favourite flowers of the period usually play some part in the design and sometimes they occupy the centre of the stage. They may be arranged in bunches, cornucopiae or vases (64), shown singly in shaped compartments, entwined round strapwork or rococo scrolls, or wreathed in garlands or festoons, but always they are boldly drawn, often with more than a hint of oriental influence, and worked in bright, naturalistic, carefully-shaded colours usually set off against a plain background of blue, yellow, brown or red. Occasionally more stylized floral forms are found, arranged in rows and worked in Hungarian or Florentine stitch. Elaborate designs of large flowers and leaves were especially favoured for embroidered carpets (62), which came back into favour at this period. Large wall-hangings were again made in canvas work too, the most notable extant examples being those from Stoke Edith[67] depicting a country house and garden and a classical scene, Lady Julia Calverley's floral pieces of 1716 at Wallington, Northumberland,[68] and two hangings with views of country houses within a floral design worked by Mary Holte of Aston Hall, Birmingham in 1744.[69]

Embroideresses now, once again, turned their attention to their clothes as well as their houses and, just as in the 16th century the same designs and techniques of linen embroidery were used both for costume and furnishing, so in the first half of the 18th century similar motifs appear on silk embroidered quilts, dresses and waistcoats, or on crewelwork hangings, bodices and petticoats. The most sumptuous effects were created by the use of bright multi-coloured silk or chenille embroidery, in flat stitches such as long and short or satin stitch, lavishly combined with couched silver or silver-gilt thread on silk or satin grounds. A typical example of the splendid sets of coverlet and pillows in this technique is that given as a wedding present in 1717 to the Rev. John Dolben, Bart. and his bride, the sister of Lord Digby (59). It bears bunches of flowers in bowls and cornucopiae ornamented in the manner of contemporary silver. Similar flowers appear on a dress of about 1730 (67), where they are combined with fine rococo ornament of strapwork and lozenge diaper patterns, and on a characteristic wide silk apron of the period (69), while a design of large leaves adorns the coat that William Morshead is said to have worn to his wedding in 1745 (68).

Much of this embroidery is technically of a very high standard and clearly the work of professionals, many of whose names have been preserved on bills in the royal accounts and elsewhere. In addition to the fine silk and metal thread embroidery already described, the professional workers produced heraldic embroidery and church furnishings, usually of velvet

[66] A chair of the first quarter of the century in the Museum (W.25–1922) bears scenes adapted from the illustrations in John Ogilby's edition of Virgil's *Aeneid*, London, 1658.

[67] Now at Montacute, Somerset; see Margaret Jourdain, "Needlework Hangings from Stoke Edith" in *Country Life Annual*, 1951, p. 81.

[68] Wingfield Digby, "Lady Julia Calverley, Embroideress" in *Connoisseur*, Vol. CXLV, 1960, pp. 82 and 169.

[69] G. C. Bainbridge, "Interesting Embroideries in Derby" in *Embroidery*, Summer, 1954, p. 56.

simply adorned with the sacred monogram or a similar device in metal thread. Although many professional embroiderers were well-known in their own day and people were able to identify their work——Mrs. Delaney, for example, makes several admiring references in the 1750s to the work of a Mrs. Jenny Glegg[70]—it is not now possible for us to do so. When the fine silk embroidery of the period is in question it is often difficult even to distinguish professional from amateur work. Sometimes amateur work is signed, however, and sometimes superlative technique betrays the professional hand or several fine pieces may be so alike in design that it seems probable that they originated in the same workshop.[71]

An example of an elaborate design which seems to be undoubtedly professional work is a coverlet (60) and matching valances and pillows adorned with flowers and strapwork in a popular contemporary colour scheme, red and yellow. Large numbers of silk embroidered coverlets bear central motifs, such as a bouquet, basket or garland of flowers or a chinoiserie bird in a contorted attitude within a garland, matching motifs in the four corners and a wide border all round of flowers, strapwork or ribbons, all set off by a background of chevrons, shell pattern, lozenges or vermicular lines worked in back or running stitches in cream or yellow silk in imitation of quilting. These coverlets are not usually padded but the silk ground is generally lined with linen, the embroidery being worked through both layers. Sometimes designs of this type were worked entirely in chain stitch, a

technique derived from Indian embroidery, or in couched knotting, as well as in the familiar flat silk stitchery. The designs often betray Indian or Persian as well as Chinese influence. Silk embroidered hangings often bore rows of flower sprigs or small bouquets, drawn either naturalistically or with an oriental flavour and worked in polychrome, monochrome or a combination of two colours such as red and green or red and yellow, or rows of figures or birds in the Chinese manner. Similar motifs may be found on dresses, jackets and stomachers and on the large caps used by men for informal wear at home. Occasionally silk embroidery even borrowed the trailing designs of branches of leaves and flowers originally used in crewelwork.

In the early 18th century crewelwork was used for jackets and dresses, coats and waistcoats as well as for hangings. The repertoire of designs was now often similar to that of silk embroidery and flat stitchery or chain stitch was often preferred to the more elaborate technique of the previous century. A characteristic mixture of blue strapwork and polychrome flowers appears on a set of hangings worked by an amateur, Rachel Corbett, in about 1729 (61). The 17th century tradition of crewelwork still persisted quite strongly, however, although oriental influences have resulted in a greater liveliness of colour and design. A typical 18th century design in this manner, dating from about 1701 (56),[72] features an exotic tree within a little palisade worked in a variety of gay colours. This gaiety also affected the heavier designs of leafy branches which are still sometimes found.[73]

[70] Lady Llanover, *ed.*, *The Autobiography and Correspondence of Mary Granville, Mrs. Delaney*, London, 1861, Vol. II, pp. 250 and 399.

[71] Cf., for instance, a yellow silk embroidered coverlet in the Museum (T.43-1962) with an almost identical example at Glynde Place, near Lewes, and a closely related coverlet in the Metropolitan Museum, New York (P. Remington, *English Domestic Needlework*, 1945, Pl. 40).

[72] It may be compared with a dated piece of similar design at Colonial Williamsburg, Virginia, see M. J. Davis, *The Art of Crewel Embroidery*, New York, 1962, p. 26.

[73] Cf. a set of bed-hangings dated 1755 (72 to F-1897), Nevinson, *Catalogue of English Domestic Embroidery*, 1950, p. 67 and Pl. LI.

Decorative quilting had begun to be popular in the 17th century but the craze for it knew no bounds in the early 18th century, when nearly all silk embroideries had backgrounds worked in imitation of it and even the sumptuous silk and metal thread coverlets had grounds worked in metal thread couched in quilting patterns. Silk petticoats were frequently quilted in floral designs, and linen jackets, waistcoats, bodices and robes were adorned with the most elaborate designs often worked in drawn fabric stitches combined with Italian quilting. In this technique motifs were outlined with parallel lines of backstitching worked through two layers of material and padded by thick, soft linen threads. Similar designs and techniques were used on linen coverlets (71), pillow-covers and linings for baby baskets, in addition to simpler quilting in stylized designs of baskets of flowers, feathers, fans or scallop shells. Quilting was generally worked in white linen or yellow or cream silk on white or cream grounds.

White quilting was popular for babies' caps, while lighter baby wear was often ornamented with delicate white embroidery, sometimes in the needlepoint technique known as "hollie" point which occurs on a number of samplers[74] of the middle years of the century. Airy white embroidery was used too by women to enhance the gay colours of their dresses. Aprons, fichus and sleeve ruffles were worked on fine muslin in delicate embroidery of chain stitch, satin stitch and drawn fabric work, with Chinoiserie (70) or elaborate formal floral designs.

Some talented and enterprising needlewomen, such as Lady Barbara North and Mrs. Delaney,[75] drew their own embroidery designs, but many more made use of the well advertised services of professional draughtsmen, haberdashers or milliners: "Miss Hare . . . sells . . . drawings of all sorts for every kind of needlework at the shortest notice." Amateur draughtsmen found themselves much in demand. Walter Gale,

a Sussex schoolmaster, for instance, not only measured out a hop-garden for Mr. Baker in 1751, but he also drew embroidery patterns for that gentleman's daughters.[76] Contemporary books of flower engravings, often expressly intended to help embroiderers, were useful sources of design and, towards the middle of the century, embroidery patterns began to appear in publications such as the *Lady's Magazine* of the early 1760s, foreshadowing the flood of printed designs which was to appear in the following century.

Soon after the middle of the 18th century fashions in embroidery began to change as lighter modes of ornament came into vogue. Bold flowers in richly coloured silks and metal threads now gave way to quieter renderings of flowers drawn in a more delicately naturalistic manner. Typical examples of later 18th-century work are a silk firescreen panel of 1792 with a spray of flowers (74) and a bed of yellow-green silk and velvet at Osterley Park embroidered with floral swags (75). For silk dresses and waistcoats too, tiny flower sprigs or delicate floral trails, often worked in chain-stitch embroidery or in chenille, heightened with metallic spangles of various shapes, now became fashionable. At this period chain stitch was usually worked with a small hook, a method said to have been introduced into Europe from China in the late 1760s.[77] The technique was known as tambour-work because the material to be embroidered was stretched in a round frame like the top of a drum (French: *tambour*). The same techniques and designs were adopted for white muslin embroidery. This became so popular by the end of the century that a cottage embroidery industry began to grow up to satisfy the demand alongside the manufacture of muslin in Western Scotland.[78]

Crewelwork hangings and silk-embroidered coverlets and pillows seem to have declined in favour after the middle of the century, though quilting remained popular. A technique which assumed prominence at

[74] King, *Samplers*, p. 9.
[75] Kendrick, *English Needlework*, 1967, p. 145.
[76] *Sussex Archaeological Collections*, Vol. IX, 1857, pp. 182 ff.
[77] According to C. G. de Saint-Aubin, *L'Art du Brodeur*, 1770.
[78] M. Swain, *The Flowerers*, London and Edinburgh, 1955.

this time was patchwork. Early pieces are usually very simple, consisting of rectangles of printed cottons joined together to make a quilt or coverlet which might be further embellished with simple embroidery and signed and dated by the worker. Even in the middle of the 18th century, however, more elaborate work is to be found. A set of hangings, dated to this period by the printed cottons of which it is made, features a shell design borrowed from quilting (72), a technique which seems to have been closely allied to patchwork from the beginning. Another design adapted from quilting was the feather pattern and patchwork coverlets were often quilted as a finishing touch. In addition the familiar patchwork in lozenges and hexagons soon appeared on the scene. Towards the end of the century there arose a fashion for cutting shapes or motifs out of printed cottons and applying them to a plain ground, a technique often combined with patchwork. Some cottons were even printed with designs specifically intended for use in this way. Both applied work and patchwork were soon adapted to picture-making, as may be seen from a mosaic coverlet bearing Napoleonic War scenes and other subjects copied from popular prints of about 1805 (76).

After about 1770 canvas work declined in favour, though a certain amount was still made in the rather delicate Chinoiserie style of the late 18th century or in geometric patterns for upholstery.

It cannot be denied that, on the whole, the later decades of the 18th century witnessed a decline in embroidery. Even the sampler, with the exception of those devoted to darning, a humbler form of needlework, had now abandoned all pretence to being a training in the finer technicalities of stitchery.[79] Stylized motifs and verses in cross stitch had now become the order of the day on the majority of samplers, although needlework seems to have been pressed into the service of the geography lesson at this time, to judge from the number of map samplers that have survived.

Another symptom of the decline of embroidery from a useful craft to a mere amusing pastime was the return to favour of the embroidered picture. Pictures were now worked on a silk ground in simple flat stitches in silk or chenille with details such as faces and hands drawn in and painted in watercolour. Popular subjects included pastoral scenes or sentimental themes such as Charlotte mourning for Werther or Fame strewing flowers on Shakespeare's tomb (77). Slavish copies of engravings were painstakingly worked in black silk or, very occasionally, in hair.

More elaborate and pretentious were the large-scale copies of paintings executed in long and short stitches in worsted which were produced by several ambitious needlewomen,[80] including Mrs. Lloyd, wife of the Dean of Norwich, Mrs. Mary Knowles[81] and Miss Morritt of Rokeby, whose work Arthur Young considered "the most elegant production of female genius".[82] Most famous of all was Miss Mary Linwood of Leicester (78),[83] who held exhibitions in London of her work, which was praised in the most extravagant terms: "The forms and expression of the figures discover the power of Michael Angelo, and the whole effect of the piece is almost magical, and beyond the power of the pencil."[84]

[79] King, *Samplers*, 1960, pp. 8–9.

[80] Kendrick, *English Needlework*, 1967, pp. 169–71.

[81] Her embroidered portrait of George III after Zoffany, dated 1780, is in the Museum's collection (160–1901). She embroidered another picture showing herself in the act of embroidering this portrait.

[82] *A 6 Months Tour through the North of England*, 1770.

[83] See *Mary Linwood*, Leicester Museums and Art Gallery. Other pictures by Mary Linwood may be seen in Leicester, while her copy of Carlo Dolci's *Salvator Mundi*, which she considered her masterpiece and bequeathed to Queen Victoria, is still in the royal collection.

[84] From *The Times*, March 28th, 1831.

19th century

An over-enthusiastic devotion to picture-making for its own sake did not lead to the raising of standards of embroidery. This was made abundantly plain in the first half of the 19th century. As early as 1804 a publisher in Berlin set about satisfying the perpetual demand for embroidery designs by issuing canvas work patterns printed in colour on squared paper. These were soon being imported into England by a Mr. Wilks of Regent Street, together with the wools for working them. By about 1830 Berlin woolwork[85] had superseded all other types of embroidery in popular favour. Suitable wools were soon being produced in Yorkshire and patterns published in magazines and embroidery books. The extent of the craze may be gauged by the phrase used by Mrs. Henry Owen in 1847 to open her *Illuminated Book of Needlework*: "Embroidery or as it is more often called Berlin woolwork. . . ." Innumerable embroidered pictures in this technique have survived, some of them being signed and dated by the worker. They reflect the sentimental taste of the times in their subject-matter: romanticized scenes of medieval life or English history, episodes from the novels of Sir Walter Scott, Biblical stories set in landscapes with palm trees and white buildings of vaguely oriental type, pet dogs on cushions or royalist themes such as copies of Winterhalter's portraits of the Queen and her family or depictions of the royal children (81).

Many Berlin woolwork designs were intended for practical use, however, as upholstery, carpets, bell-pulls, bags or slippers. From the beginning the favourite designs were floral. In the 1820s and 1830s a fairly restrained style prevailed and flowers were often combined with the revived rococo or gothic ornament of the period on light-coloured grounds (80). In the 1840s, however, restraint was thrown to the winds and bold, lush flowers such as full-blown roses or heavy, waxy lilies, were depicted in as three-dimensional manner as possible in brightly-coloured wools against a black, red or blue ground (79).

For the most part a simple technique using only cross and tent stitches was favoured, though there survive from the middle of the century a number of samplers, perhaps worked by skilled needlewomen for the guidance of amateurs,[86] featuring more elaborate types of stitchery. These are, however, rarely found on practical embroidery and are generally used only for geometric designs. Two innovations which came into Berlin woolwork around the middle of the century were the use of beads and of raised pile. A typical example of beadwork is a small hand-screen of about 1860 (82) with a design in the revived classical style of the period in grey and white beads against a blue ground.

Further evidence for the all-pervading influence of Berlin woolwork in the first half of the 19th century is the appearance of three-dimensionally shaded motifs on the samplers made by little girls. Otherwise samplers continued the tradition established in the late 18th century, until their final decline and disappearance during the second half of the 19th century.[87]

For refinement of design and technique in the early 19th century we must turn to the work of a new class of professionals, in the cottage embroidery industry now firmly established in Western Scotland and Northern Ireland. The best-known surviving examples of the Ayrshire work[88] they produced are the ubiquitous christening robes adorned with elaborate patterns in satin and outline stitches enriched with cutwork and delicate needlepoint fillings (83). Similar embroidery was used to embellish the muslin dresses, caps, fichus and pelerines which enjoyed a great popularity up to the end of the 1830s. After this time Ayrshire work was gradually superseded by the rather coarser "Broderie Ang-

[85] B. Morris, *Victorian Embroidery*, London, 1962, pp. 19-30.
[86] King, *Samplers*, p. 10.
[87] *Ibid.*, pp. 9-10.
[88] Swain, *op. cit.*; Morris, *op. cit.*, pp. 32-40.

[89] Morris, *op. cit.*, pp. 38–40.
[90] *Ibid.*, pp. 40–1.
[91] Anne Buck, "The Countryman's Smock" in *Folk-Life*, Vol. 1, 1963, p. 16.
[92] Morris, *op. cit.*, pp. 51–2, 61–2.
[93] *Ibid.*, pp. 70–85; Christine Risley, *Machine Embroidery*, London, 1961, ch. 1.
[94] Two pieces of Houldsworth's work acquired by the Museum from the Dublin exhibition are a satin band embroidered in shaded silks (796–1854) and an embroidered green baize tablecloth (795–1854).

laise"[89] in which patterns were built up from series of round or oval holes edged with overcasting or buttonholing. An even heavier type of whitework of the mid-19th century was "Mountmellick work",[90] which is said to have originated in Ireland and which featured floral designs worked in thick cotton on a strong cotton ground.

In the first decades of the 19th century costume was sometimes embellished with classical designs worked in coloured silks or in metal threads. Later on rather stereotyped designs of flowers drawn in a simple fashion appeared in bags, shawls, aprons and sometimes dresses. They were worked in polychrome in flat silk stitchery or with raised effects achieved by the use of narrow shaded ribbons, light gauzy fabrics or even straw. Similar designs were sometimes worked in hair on pocket-books, needlecases and handkerchiefs as mementoes. In the 1850s rather crudely drawn flowers worked in very bright colours on light materials such as gauze or net were popular for evening wear.

A completely different type of costume embroidery occurs on the smocks worn by country people at this time. These heavy linen garments of simple cut were embellished with ornamental stitchery on the gathers at front and back and on the sleeves, and with patterns in feather, chain and other simple stitches on shoulders, collar and cuffs (84). Many of them were produced in rural workshops and, though certain regional differences may be detected in cut or colour, the embroidery generally affords no guidance to the provenance of the smock or the trade of the wearer.[91]

Quilting had by now become a traditional country craft, particularly in the north country and in Wales, where characteristic designs of two distinct varieties had become standardized.[92] Patchwork was still beloved of many needlewomen as well as picture-making in mosaic patchwork or applied work (85).

Although standards of design and technique were generally low, the demand for embroidered costume and furnishings grew steadily during the early 19th century and it was not long before an attempt was made to meet it by the use of machinery. In 1828 Josué Heilmann of Mulhouse invented a machine which produced embroidery by means of a row of needles with an eye in the centre and a point at each end. The needles were pushed and pulled through material stretched in a frame, and caught and held by pincers as they emerged. Designs were copied with the aid of a pantograph attached to the machine.[93] The English patent rights of this machine were acquired by Henry Houldsworth of Manchester, who modified it and soon began to produce sprigged dress materials. He showed examples of dress and furnishing embroideries at the Great Exhibition of 1851 and the Dublin Exhibition of 1853.[94] The main development of the machine, however, took place in Switzerland and Germany, where it was used to produce enormous quantities of white embroidery which drove hand-made whitework off the market after the middle of the century. Further advances included the invention of the shuttle or *schifflé* machine by Isaac Groebli in 1865. In this the principle of the original embroidery machine was combined with the use of a continuous thread as in the domestic sewing machine. After this invention had been perfected, the machine embroidery industry spread rapidly. It was taken up by several firms in England and Scotland in the last decades of the century, and apart from court and *couture* dresses, virtually all embroidered costume from this time onwards was produced by machinery. Final developments soon after 1900 were the adaptation of the lock-stitch and chain-stitch sewing machines to the production of embroidery on a commercial scale.

It was inevitable that there should be a reaction against both the stereotyped products of machinery and the low level of hand embroidery. This began as early as the 1840s under the auspices of various architects who promoted a revival of church needlework. They included A. W. Pugin, who himself made designs for vestments and G. E. Street, through whose influence the Ladies' Ecclesiastical Embroidery Society was founded in 1854.[95] The pieces produced at this time were in a revived medieval style and used the medieval applied work technique. Other architects took an interest in church embroidery in the 1860s, but it was William Morris whose work was to have the most far-reaching effects on embroidery in general.

Morris, who had worked for Street, began by designing embroideries for his own home, the Red House, in about 1860. These pieces[96] were worked by members of his family in techniques learned by the painstaking unravelling of old embroidery, particularly crewelwork. Later Morris, often in co-operation with Sir Edward Burne-Jones, went on to design many large-scale embroideries such as hangings and coverlets with pictorial or bold flower and leaf designs (86). These were executed by skilled needlewomen for the firm of Morris, Marshall, Faulkner & Co., founded in 1861.[97] Much of the work was carried out in crewel wools or silks in long and short stitches closely arranged to cover the whole surface of the ground material, but sometimes more intricate stitchery derived from 17th century crewelwork was used. In the later decades of the century many designs were made for the firm by Morris's daughter May and by J. H. Dearle.

Amateur needlewomen were able to buy designs and materials from the firm and Morris's theories on embroidery design were destined to have a far-reaching effect. In a lecture, "Hints on Pattern Designing", in 1881 he said, "It is a quite delightful idea to cover a piece of linen cloth with roses, jonquils and tulips done quite natural with the needle and we can't go too far in that direction if we only remember the needs of our material and the nature of our craft in general: these demand that our roses and the like, however unmistakably roses, shall be quaint and naïve to the last degree, and also since we are using especially beautiful materials, that we shall make the most of them and not forget that we are gardening with silk and gold thread."

These ideas made an immediate appeal and amateurs eagerly adopted this new "gardening" which, under the name of "Art Needlework", dominated the later decades of the 19th century as Berlin woolwork had the earlier (87). Art Needlework was promoted by numerous societies established in the 1870s and 1880s, including the Royal School of Art Needlework,[98] by a spate of publications and by architects and designers who furnished designs for domestic as well as ecclesiastical use. The emphasis was now once more on embroidery for practical purposes, for curtains, hangings, *portières*, screens, bedcovers, cushions and tablecloths.

One aspect of Art Needlework was a revival of crewelwork both in contemporary designs and in adaptations of 17th century patterns. Whatever the design, the embroidery was usually worked in a soft range of colours imitating the results of two centuries of fading rather than the original strong colours of the 17th century work. A certain amount of canvas work in copies of late 17th and early 18th century designs in similar "art" colours was also made at this time.

Very popular too were floral designs, featuring marigolds, irises, slender lilies or wild roses quite different from the Berlin woolwork flowers, delicately drawn and worked in silks and silver-gilt thread on silk grounds. A typical example, of most meticulous workmanship, is a flower-bedecked screen panel made in 1899 (87). Sometimes the designs reflected the current enthusiasm for things Japanese. Related types of needlework are Leek embroidery, that is, the em-

[95] Morris, *op. cit.*, pp. 85-8.
[96] *Ibid.*, p. 96.
[97] *Ibid.*, pp. 97-112.
[98] *Ibid.*, pp. 113-19.

bellishment by stitchery of designs printed on silk tussore,[99] and Anglo-Indian embroidery, stitchery on cotton printed with designs of Indian inspiration.[100]

Two other features of this late 19th century revival of embroidery were closely linked together: the renewal of interest in old embroidery of all kinds and the attempt to revive dying rural industries or to create new ones. Both were expressions of revulsion against the machine and all its products, a feeling quite unknown to the early Victorians. There was, for example, a revival of interest in smocking. Collections of old smocks were amassed and the technique was used for ornamenting blouses and children's dresses. Drawn-thread work enjoyed a revival and Mountmellick work was popular again as was a type of cutwork known as Richelieu work with designs based, somewhat remotely, on 16th and 17th century models.[101] Amongst the rural industries established at this period was the Langdale Linen Industry of Westmorland, devoted to the production of linen cutwork in *reticella* patterns of the 16th century.[102] In contrast to this, the Haslemere Peasant Industries, set up in 1896 by Godfrey Blount,[103] produced applied work in pictorial or simple stylized designs often with a marked contemporary flavour.

One of the most significant and original developments at the end of the century took place at Glasgow School of Art.[104] Here an entirely new type of embroidery was evolved, with stylized designs in the Art Nouveau manner carried out in simple stitchery on linen or in applied work. A characteristic example is a cushion cover of about 1900 (88) by Jessie R. Newbery, who was mainly responsible for this development. Her work was carried still further by Ann Macbeth, who succeeded her as head of the embroidery department in 1908. Most of the students trained at Glasgow were destined to teach in Scottish schools and Ann Macbeth evolved and promulgated the idea of encouraging all needleworkers, even the youngest children, to make their own designs on the basis of the stitchery or the materials used. She placed great importance on simplicity both in design and materials, preferring "linen, cotton and crash, and the many beautiful fabrics of a cheap kind that modern scientific manufacturing furnishes, to the exclusion of the costly, but really less artistic, silks and satins considered by a past generation superlatively beautiful." These were revolutionary ideas indeed, destined to have a profound influence on embroidery in the following century.

20th century

Much of the embroidery of the present century developed along lines established in the later 19th century. For a long time Art Needlework continued to exert its spell and some fine work in this manner was produced in the first two decades of the century. Typical examples are a set of curtains (89) produced in about 1905 for Fanhams Hall by the Royal School of Needlework. After this period, however, the tradition degenerated and this resulted in the production of a plethora of vapid designs disseminated through printed transfers and executed in a limited range of simple stitches. Commercially produced designs for canvas work, which remained one of the most popular techniques, soon became equally banal.

In contrast the revival of techniques of fine stitchery continued to develop fruitfully. Characteristic of work of this type is a fine whitework quilt (90) in a drawn fabric technique and a design borrowed from the early 18th century. It was made by Mrs. Arthur Newall, who established a rural embroidery industry at Fisherton-de-la-Mere in 1902.[105]

[99] *Ibid.*, p. 120.
[100] *Ibid.*, p. 121.
[101] *Ibid.*, p. 45.
[102] *Ibid.*, pp. 47–8.
[103] *Ibid.*, pp. 68–9.
[104] *Ibid.*, pp. 147–48, 157–58.
[105] *Ibid.*, pp. 48–9.

One of the most important and influential advocates of skilled stitchery in the 1920s and 1930s was Mrs. Archibald Christie, whose book *Samplers and Stitches* was a model for many later publications. Mrs. Christie's own fine and meticulous techniques of embroidery were firmly based on the devoted study of historical pieces, a study which came to fruition with the publication of her monumental book *English Medieval Embroidery* in 1938.

Encouraged by such examples and by the work of bodies like the Embroiderers' Guild, Women's Institutes, Townswomen's Guilds and, in Scotland, the Needlework Development Scheme,[106] high standards of skill were once more attained by students of needlework and by amateurs working at home. Techniques such as blackwork were lovingly revived, while others, such as patchwork and beadwork which had remained popular, were refined and improved. Countrywomen still practising the traditional craft of quilting,[107] were now encouraged to improve their techniques and designs by bodies such as the Rural Industries Bureau, which also helped them to find a market for their work. The emphasis was generally placed on fine embroidery for practical use. Designs tended to rely heavily on ideas borrowed from the past and to be on the whole rather unadventurous, although since the Second World War many efforts have been made to introduce a more contemporary flavour into the design of patterns meant to be executed in fine stitchery. This is a particularly noticeable development in church embroidery. Quantities of kneelers have been produced in fine canvas work with a greatly enlarged repertoire of stitches and skilled work in couched metal threads has assumed a new importance.[108]

The ideas originated by the Glasgow School of Art have, on the other hand, given rise to a totally new conception of embroidery. Here the main emphasis has been on creativity, generally based on simple techniques allowing for speed of execution to preserve the freshness of the original idea. Embroidery of this type was pioneered in the 1920s and 1930s by Mrs. Rebecca Crompton. She was particularly attracted by the applied work techniques used by the Glasgow School and she used them with great effect in the making of embroidered pictures which were completely contemporary in feeling (91). Mrs. Crompton was also one of the first to exploit the possibilities of sewing and embroidery machines for creative embroidery.

The movement for creative embroidery in contemporary designs has gathered impetus steadily since the Second World War. Techniques such as applied work have been successfully used to create church vestments and furnishings which accord well with the modern buildings for which they are intended. Machine embroidery, too, has proved particularly well adapted for practical use on costume, cushion covers and tablecloths. Generally speaking, however, the emphasis of this movement seems to have shifted towards the production of purely decorative pieces such as embroidered pictures, as if embroidery were trying to move away from the sphere of applied art into that of fine art. Picture-making in machine embroidery is popular (93), while techniques of applied work, beadwork and simple forms of stitchery have been combined in the fabric collage (92). In some recent work, notably that produced by students of the Glasgow School of Art,[109] stitchery of any but the most rudimentary variety has been abandoned, the finished result now depending on the skilful blending of materials of different colours and textures only lightly attached to the background. It may, indeed, be doubted whether such pieces can legitimately be described as embroidery any more. They certainly represent the most extreme development so far seen in the direction of freedom of expression in this medium.

[106] R. Oddy, *Needlework Development Scheme*, Edinburgh, 1965. Many of the embroideries made for the Scheme are now in the Department of Circulation, Victoria and Albert Museum.
[107] Helen E. Fitzrandolph and M. Doriel Hay, *The Rural Industries of England and Wales. A Survey made on behalf of the Agricultural Economics Research Institute*, Oxford, Vol. III, 'Decorative Crafts and Rural Potteries', Oxford, 1927.
[108] B. Dean, *Ecclesiastical Embroidery*, London, 1958.
[109] Cf. an embroidered picture of poppies in the Museum (Circ. 181–1963).

Select Bibliography

Victoria & Albert Museum Publications

Catalogue of English Ecclesiastical Embroideries of the XIII to XVI Centuries. 4th ed. 1930.

NEVINSON, J. L. *Catalogue of English Domestic Embroidery of the 16th and 17th Centuries.* 2nd ed. 1950.

KING, D. *Samplers.* 1960.

WADE, N. V. *Basic Stitches of Embroidery.* 2nd ed. 1966.

Notes on Applied Work and Patchwork. 1938.

Notes on Quilting. 1932.

PICTURE BOOKS

Elizabethan Embroidery. 1948.
Flowers in English Embroidery. 1947.
Gospel Stories in English Embroidery. 1963.

Books

BATTISCOMBE, C. R., ed. *The Relics of St. Cuthbert.* Oxford, 1956.

CARDIFF: National Museum of Wales. PAYNE, F. G. *Guide to the Collection of Samplers and Embroideries.* Cardiff, 1939.

CHRISTIE, *Mrs.* A. G. I. *Samplers and Stitches.* London, 1920.

CHRISTIE, *Mrs.* A. G. I. *English Medieval Embroidery.* Oxford, 1938.

COLBY, A. *Patchwork.* London, 1958.

COLBY, A. *Samplers.* London, 1964.

CROMPTON, R. *Modern Design in Embroidery.* London, 1936.

DAVENPORT, C. *English Embroidered Bookbindings.* London, 1899.

DEAN, B. *Ecclesiastical Embroidery.* London, 1958.

ENTHOVEN, J. *The Stitches of Creative Embroidery.* New York, 1964.

FITZRANDOLPH, M. *Traditional Quilting.* London, 1954.

GRAY, J. *Machine Embroidery.* London, 1963.

HACKENBROCH, Y. *English and other Needlework, Tapestries and Textiles in the Untermeyer Collection.* Cambridge, Mass., 1960.

HAKE, E. *English Quilting, Old and New.* London, 1937.

HOLFORD, C. *A Chat about the Broderers' Company.* London, 1910.

HOWARD, C. *Inspiration for Embroidery.* London, 1966.

JOURDAIN, M. *English Secular Embroidery.* London, 1910.

KENDRICK, A. F. *English Decorative Fabrics of the 16th to 18th Centuries.* London, 1934.

KENDRICK, A. F. *English Needlework.* 2nd ed. London, 1967.

MORRIS, B. *Victorian Embroidery.* London, 1962.

RISLEY, C. *Machine Embroidery.* London, 1961.

SELIGMAN, G., and HUGHES, T. *Domestic Needlework.* London, 1926.

STENTON, Sir F. M., ed. *The Bayeux Tapestry.* London, 1957.

SWAIN, M. *The Flowerers.* London and Edinburgh, 1955.

SWANSON, M., and MACBETH, A. *Educational Needlecraft.* London, 1913.

WINGFIELD DIGBY, G. F. *Elizabethan Embroidery.* London, 1963.

ZULUETA, F. de. *Embroideries by Mary Stuart and Elizabeth Talbot at Oxburgh Hall, Norfolk.* Oxford (privately printed), 1923.

Articles

BRETT, K. B. "English Crewelwork Curtains in the Royal Ontario Museum" in *Embroidery*, Vol. 16, No. 1, Spring, 1965, p. 13.

BUCK, A. "The Countryman's Smock" in *Folk-life*, Vol. 1, 1963, p. 16.

CABOT, N. G. "Pattern Sources for Scriptural Subjects in Tudor and Stuart Embroideries" in *Bulletin of the Needle and Bobbin Club*, Vol. XXX, Nos. 1 and 2, 1946, p. 3.

CALBERG, M. "Tissus et Broderies attribués aux Saintes Harlinde et Relinde" in *Bulletin de la Société Royale d'Archéologie de Bruxelles*, October, 1951, p. 1.

IRWIN, J. C. "Origins of the 'Oriental Style' in English Decorative Art" in *Burlington Magazine*, Vol. XCVII, 1955, p. 106.

JOURDAIN, M. "Needlework Hangings from Stoke Edith" in *Country Life Annual*, 1951, p. 81.

KING, D. "The Earliest Dated Sampler" in *Connoisseur*, Vol. CXLIX, 1962, p. 234.

NEVINSON, J. L. "English Embroidered Costume, Elizabeth and James I" in *Connoisseur*, Vol. XCVII, 1936, pp. 25 and 40.

NEVINSON, J. L. "Peter Stent and John Overton, Publishers of Embroidery Designs" in *Apollo*, Vol. XXI, 1936, p. 279.

NEVINSON, J. L. "English Domestic Embroidery Patterns of the 16th and 17th Centuries" in *Walpole Society*, Vol. XXVIII, 1939–40, p. 1.

NEVINSON, J. L. "The Embroidered Miniature Portraits of Charles I" in *Apollo*, Vol. LXXXII, 1965, p. 310.

WARDLE, P. "English Pictorial Embroidery of the 17th Century" in *Antiques International*, ed. P. C. Wilson, London, 1966, p. 276.

WINGFIELD DIGBY, G. F. "Lady Julia Calverley, Embroideress" in *Connoisseur*, Vol. CXLV, 1960, pp. 82 and 169.

Exhibition Catalogues

METROPOLITAN MUSEUM OF ART, New York. REMINGTON, P. *English Domestic Needlework of the XVI, XVII and XVIII Centuries.* 1945.

MUSEUM AND ART GALLERY, Birmingham. *British Embroidery, 13th–19th Century.* 1959.

CASTLE MUSEUM, Norwich. *Needlework in East Anglia.* 1961.

VICTORIA AND ALBERT MUSEUM AND ARTS COUNCIL OF GREAT BRITAIN, London. KING, D. *Opus Anglicanum.* 1963.

ROYAL SCOTTISH MUSEUM, Edinburgh. ODDY, R. *Catalogue of Embroideries from Needlework Development Scheme.* 1965.

List of Illustrations

8. Panel from a Burse, 1310–40 (detail)

The Coronation of the Virgin.
On the other panel, *The Crucifixion*
Linen embroidered with coloured silks and silver-gilt thread in split stitch, underside couching and laid and couched work.

T.62–1936 (Neg. No. 74995)

9. The Marnhull Orphrey, 1315–35 (detail)

Christ carrying the cross.
The orphrey bears the arms of the Wokyndon family.
Linen embroidered with coloured silks and silver-gilt and silver thread in split stitch, underside couching and laid and couched work.
Given by the National Art Collections Fund. T.231–1936 (Neg. No. 74251)

10. The Butler-Bowdon Cope, 1330–50 (detail)

The Adoration of the Magi.
Velvet embroidered with coloured silks, silver-gilt and silver thread, pearls, green beads and small gold rings in split stitch, underside and surface couching, laid and couched work and raised work.
Bought with the aid of the National Art Collections Fund and private donors. T.36–1955 (Neg. No. Q.1258)

11. Cope Orphrey, 1340–70 (detail)

An Angel and St. Catherine.
Velvet embroidered with coloured silks and silver-gilt and silver thread in split stitch, underside couching and raised work.

176–1889 (Neg. No. 37439)

12. Apparels of Albs, 1320–40 (detail)

The Annunciation.
The apparels bear the arms of Bardolf and another family.
Velvet embroidered with coloured silks and silver-gilt and silver thread in split stitch, underside couching, laid and couched work and raised work.
Given by Mr. Ralph Oakden. 8218–1863 (Neg. No. X. 1408)

13. Chasuble Orphrey, 1390–1420 (detail)

The Nativity of the Virgin.
The orphrey applied to a chasuble of Italian brocaded silk.
Linen embroidered with coloured silks and silver-gilt and silver thread in split stitch, underside couching, laid and couched work and raised work.
Given by Mrs. Gordon-Canning. T.27–1922 (Neg. No. X. 1005)

14. Chasuble with Orphreys, 1434–45 (detail)

The Crucifixion with the Virgin and St. John.
Above: *God the Father with the Holy Ghost as a dove.*
The orphrey bears the arms of Henry de Beauchamp, Duke of Warwick (d. 1445), after his marriage to Lady Cecily Neville in 1434.
The chasuble of Italian velvet brocaded in silver-gilt thread.
The orphreys, linen embroidered with coloured silks and silver-gilt and silver thread in split stitch, couched work and raised work.

402–1907 (Neg. No. F.D.24)

15. Hood of a Cope, 1460–90

The Virgin and Child enthroned.
Linen embroidered with coloured silks and silver-gilt and silver thread in split, brick and long and short stitches and couched work.
Given by Sir Charles and Lady Walston. T.46–1914 (Neg. No. Y.709)

16. Cope, early 16th century (back)

The Assumption of the Virgin, and seraphim. On the hood: *Christ blessing.*
Cope of silk damask, the hood and orphrey of velvet, embroidered with gilt thread and coloured silks in split and brick stitches with laid and couched work on linen, and applied.

230–1879 (Neg. No. 37451)

17. Fragment, 1470–1500

Henry and Thomas Smyth and their wives; identified by inscriptions asking for prayers.
Linen embroidered with coloured silks and silver-gilt thread in split stitch and couched work and applied to velvet; sequins.

T.194-1911 (Neg. No. 35237)

18. Altar Frontal, 1535–55 (detail)

Ralph Nevill, fourth Earl of Westmorland, and his seven sons; above, two later shields.
The frontal also bears *Christ on the Cross between the Virgin and St. John;* on the left, *Lady Catherine Stafford and her thirteen daughters.* The couple were married in 1523.
Linen, embroidered with coloured silks and silver-gilt and silver thread in split brick and satin stitches, couched work and raised work, and applied to velvet.

35–1888 (Neg. No. 29326)

19. Chalice Veil, 16th century

In the centre the inscription UNTO GOD GIF PRIS; around the border the beginning of a metrical version of Psalm 51.
Linen embroidered with pink silk and silver thread in satin and hem stitches.

Given by the Rev. Daniel Haigh. 1415–1874 (Neg. No. 37402)

20. Bed-tester, mid-16th century (detail)

The tester bears the arms of Wentworth impaling Glemham.
Italian crimson silk and ivory silk damask embroidered with coloured silks, silk cord and metal threads in laid and applied work with French knots.

T.235-1928 (Neg. No. 61552)

21. The Gifford Table Carpet, mid-16th century (detail)

The arms of Gifford within a wreath of flowers.
Linen canvas embroidered with coloured wools in tent stitch.

Bought with the aid of the National Art Collections Fund. T.151-1930 (Neg. No. 59757)

22. The Bradford Table Carpet, late 16th century (detail)

Linen canvas embroidered with coloured silks in tent stitch.

Bought with the aid of the National Art Collections Fund. T.134-1928 (Neg. No. Y.252)

23. Long Cushion Cover, mid-16th century

The cushion cover bears arms attributed to John Warneford of Sevenhampton, Wiltshire, and his wife Susanna Yates.
Linen canvas embroidered with coloured silks in tent stitch.

Given by Mrs. Nina D. Cotton in memory of Captain Francis Cotton, R.I.M. T.120-1932 (Neg. No. 67991)

24. Long Cushion Cover, late 16th century

Linen, embroidered with coloured silks and silver-gilt and silver thread in tent, cross, long-armed cross and stem stitches and laid work, and applied to black velvet.
Lined with green silk damask and edged with fringe, and tassels of green silk and silver-gilt thread.

T.80-1946 (Neg. No. 21140)

25. Square Cushion Cover, late 16th century

Satin embroidered with coloured silks, silver-gilt thread and metal strip in satin stitch and couched work.

T.21-1923 (Neg. No. 53010)

26. Fragment of a Hanging, late 16th century (detail)

Black velvet applied to red woollen cloth with couched yellow silk cord and French knots.

Given anonymously. T.90-1926 (Neg. No. 76935)

27. Bed Valances, late 16th century

Cynaras and Myrrha, Venus and Adonis.
Linen canvas embroidered with coloured wools and silks in tent stitch and raised work.

879-1904 (Neg. No. F.J. 2343)

28a–c. Panels from the Oxburgh Hangings, 1570

Embroidered by Mary, Queen of Scots, and Elizabeth, Countess of Shrewsbury.

(a) *An elephant.* Copied from an illustration in Conrad Gesner, *Icones Animalium*, Zurich, 1560.

T.33GG–1955 (Neg. No. F.H.1501)

(b) *A flowering plant* from the Cavendish Hanging, monogram "E S"; border inscribed VERA VIRTVS PERICVLVM AFFECTAT (True courage seeks danger).

T.30-1955 (Neg. No. N.840)

(c) *Feathers falling round an armillary sphere,* with the motto LAS PENNAS PASSAN Y QVEDA LA SPERANZA (Sorrows pass but hope abides).
In the border the arms of England, Scotland, France and Spain and emblems copied from Claude Paradin, *Devises Heroïques*, Lyon, 1557.

T.33-1955 (Neg. No. F.H.1500)

Linen canvas, embroidered with coloured silks and silver-gilt thread in cross, tent and long-armed cross stitches, and applied to green velvet embellished with couched cord.

Given by the National Art Collections Fund.

29. Cover, late 16th century

The Shepheard Buss.
The emblems and some of the rebuses copied from Claude Paradin, *Devises Heroïques*, Lyon, 1557.
Linen embroidered with black silk in stem, back and satin stitches, speckling and couched work.
Border of bobbin lace.

T.219-1953 (Neg. No. 33039)

30. Pillow Cover, second half 16th century

From a set of two pillow covers and a long cover.
Linen embroidered with black silk in back, chain, cord, braid and buttonhole stitches.

T.81-1924 (Neg. No. 76263)

31. Pillow Cover, late 16th century

One of a set of four.
Linen embroidered with coloured silks and silver-gilt and silver thread in chain, square double chain, stem, plaited braid and buttonhole stitch, detached buttonhole fillings and couched work.

Acquired with the aid of Lord and Lady Melchett, Mr. and Mrs. F. H. Cook, Sir F. H. Richmond, Mr. S. Goetze, Professor and Mrs. P. E. Newberry, Mr. W. J. Holt. T.114-1928 (Neg. No. 60329)

32. Woman's Jacket, c.1600 (back)

Silk embroidered with coloured silks and silver-gilt and silver thread and spangles in satin and basket stitches and couched work.

173-1869 (Neg. No. 47531)

33. Man's Nightcap, late 16th century

Linen embroidered with silver-gilt and silver thread in chain and plaited braid stitches and knots.
Edged with silver-gilt bobbin lace with spangles.

T.75-1954 (Neg. No. N.615)

34. Woman's Hood, late 16th century

Linen embroidered with black silk in stem and double-coral stitches and speckling.
Border of bobbin lace.

Given by Mrs. Head. T.135-1924 (Neg. No. 54455)

35. Woman's Coif, late 16th century

Linen embroidered with white linen thread in chain and darning stitches with cutwork and needlepoint fillings.
Border of bobbin lace.

T.69-1938 (Neg. No. 79306)

36. Purses and Pincushion, late 16th–early 17th century

Left: Purse and pincushion. Canvas embroidered with coloured silks and silver thread in tent and chain stitches.
Plaited silk drawstrings, cord and tassel.

316 and A-1898

Top right: Purse. Canvas embroidered with coloured silks and silver-gilt and silver thread in tent, gobelin and plaited braid stitches. Plaited drawstrings and tassels in pink silk and silver thread.

Bequeathed by Miss W. M. Bompas. T.87-1935

Bottom right: Purse in the form of a bunch of grapes. Silk embroidered with coloured silks and metal thread in detached buttonhole stitch with padded work.

T.172-1921 (Neg. No. 76781)

37. Woman's Mitten, late 16th–early 17th century

One of a pair said to have been given to Margaret Edgcumbe, wife of Sir Edward Denny, by Queen Elizabeth I.
Crimson velvet and white satin embroidered with coloured silks and silver-gilt and silver thread in long and short and satin stitches and couched work. The edges bound with gilt braid.

Given by Sir Edward Denny, Bart. 1507-1882 (Neg. No. 77027)

38. Sampler, 1598

Signed JANE BOSTOCKE 1598 and inscribed
ALICE LEE WAS BORNE THE 23 OF NOVEMBER
BEING TWESDAY IN THE AFTER NOONE 1596.
Linen embroidered with coloured silks and silver-
gilt and silver thread, seed pearls and black beads
in back, Algerian eye, satin, chain, ladder, button-
hole and detached buttonhole, coral and two-sided
Italian cross stitches, couched work, speckling and
French knots.

T.190–1960 (Neg. No. V. 1914)

39. Long Cushion Cover, early 17th century

Signed MARY HVLTON. In the centre the arms of
James I and initials I R.
Linen canvas embroidered with coloured silks and
wools and silver-gilt thread in tent, plaited and
long-armed cross stitches.

816–1893 (Neg. No. 31707)

40. Pillow Cover, early 17th century (detail)

Cain and Abel, Noah building the Ark
One of a set of four.
Linen embroidered with coloured silks and silver-
gilt thread in stem, chain, back and cross stitches
with decorative fillings and speckling. From the
Abingdon Collection.

*Acquired with the help of Lord and Lady Melchett, Mr. and Mrs.
F. H. Cook, Sir F. H. Richmond, Mr. S. Goetze, Professor and
Mrs. P. E. Newberry, Mr. W. J. Holt.* T.116–1928 (Neg. No.
60331)

41. Book-Cover, 1613 (detail)

Jonah and the Whale.
The book is a Geneva Bible of 1610 bearing the
inscription ELIZABETH ILLINGWORTHE IS THE
TRUE OWNER OF THIS BIBLE.
Linen canvas embroidered with coloured silks in
tent stitch.

Acquired with the funds of the Bryan Bequest. T.134–1929 (Neg.
No. 62180)

42. Chalice Veil, second quarter 17th century

The sacred monogram and instruments of the
Passion.
Linen embroidered with red silk in stem, braid,
double-running and buttonhole stitches.

T.1–1914 (Neg. No. 38506)

43. Picture, 1637

The Adoration of the Shepherds.
One of a set.
Inscribed on the back EDMUND HARRISON IM-
BROIDERER TO KING CHARLES MADE THEIS
ANNO DONI. 1637.
Linen embroidered with coloured silks and silver-
gilt and silver thread in couched work (*or nué*), long
and short, split, brick and satin stitches.

Acquired with the funds of the Murray Bequest. T.147–1930 (Neg.
No. 28988)

44. Embroidered Shirt, c.1630 (detail)

Four of the twenty-four motifs copied from Richard
Shorleyker's *A Schole-House for the Needle*, 1624.
Linen embroidered with pink silk in stem stitch,
the seams covered with a line of cross stitch.
Trimmed with bobbin lace.

T.2–1956 (Neg. No. 51139)

45. Woman's Bodice, c.1630

Linen and cotton twill embroidered with red wool in stem, long and short and coral stitches and French knots.

T.124–1938 (Neg. No. 71920)

46. Bed Hanging, mid-17th century (detail)

One of a set of four.
Cotton and linen twill weave embroidered with red wool in stem and satin stitches, speckling and French knots.

T.165–1930 (Neg. No. 65072)

47. Picture or Long Cushion Cover, mid-17th century

Abraham and the Angels.
Linen canvas embroidered with coloured wools and silks in tent stitch.

Given by Lieut. Col. H. F. C. Lewin, R.E. 443–1865 (Neg. No. 38132)

48. Beadwork Jewel Case, 1673 (Lid)

Signed MARTHA EDLIN and dated 1673.
Padded lid covered with white satin and embroidered with glass beads and coloured silks in tent and rococo stitches.
Lined with pink satin.

Bequeathed by Sir Frederick Richmond, Bart. T.41–1954 (Neg. No. F.G.357)

49. Upholstered Chair, c.1685

From Drayton House, Northamptonshire.
Canvas embroidered with coloured wools and silks in tent, Hungarian, long and short, split and satin stitches.

W.34–1950 (Neg. No. Z.167)

50. Upholstered Chair, 1641–55

The shield on the back bears the arms of Hill of Spaxton Yarde and Pounnsford, Somerset, impaling Gurdon of Assington Hall, Suffolk and Letton, Norfolk. For the marriage of Roger Hill (d.1655) to his second wife Abigail Gurdon in 1641.
Linen canvas embroidered with coloured wools and silks in tent and cross stitches.

W.124–1937 (Neg. No. 77444)

51. Box, 1692

Initialled P M (For Parnell Mackett).
Pine-wood veneered with king-wood, with inserted panels of linen embroidered with coloured silks in rococo and double-running stitches.

T.6–1926 (Neg. No. F.H.2051)

52. Upholstered Chair. Frame, c.1675. Upholstery, c.1730

One of a set.
The coverings appear to have been originally intended for chairs with higher, shaped backs.
Yellow satin decorated with knotted red silk cord in couched work.

H.H.152-c–1 (Neg. No. H.295)

53. Hanging, second half 17th century

One of a set of six from a house in Hatton Garden.
Linen canvas embroidered with coloured wools in tent, brick, cross, crosslet and rococo stitches, couched work and French knots.

521–1896 (Neg. No. 30610)

54. Coverlet, 1692–1707

Part of a complete set of bed furniture made for George Melville (1636–1707) created 1st Earl of Melville in 1690. His initials G M with an earl's coronet appear on both the coverlet and the bed-head and on the valances.
White, Chinese silk damask decorated with couched crimson braid.

Given by the Rt. Hon. Earl of Leven. W.35–1949 (Neg. No. G.789)

55. Hanging, c.1696 (detail)

One of a set, of which one, now in the Royal Ontario Museum, bears the date 1696.
Linen and cotton twill embroidered with coloured wools in stem, long and short, chain, buttonhole, satin, Roumanian, coral, detached buttonhole and chain stitches with French knots and speckling.

T.166–1961 (Neg. No. Y.499)

56. Bed Hanging, c.1701 (detail)

There is a valance to match the hanging.
Cotton and linen twill weave embroidered with coloured wools in brick and stem stitches with bullion and French knots.

Given by Alfred Williams Hearn. T.172–1923 (Neg. No. 32824)

57. Coverlet, 1694 (detail)

Above the central medallion, a shield bearing the arms of Thurston of Challock, Kent, quartering Woodward; below, the name SARAH THURSTONE and the date 1694. A similar coverlet is in the Fitzwilliam Museum, Cambridge.
Silk embroidered with coloured silks and silver thread in stem, long and short stitches and French and bullion knots with couched work.

T.223–1953 (Neg. No. P.1044)

58. Chinoiserie Panel, c.1700

Linen canvas embroidered with coloured wools and some silk in tent stitch, the faces and other details slightly padded.

T.71–1949 (Neg. No. K.1519)

59. Coverlet, c.1717

Part of a set of coverlet and pillows given as a wedding present in 1717 to the Rev. John Dolben, Bart., and his bride, the sister of Lord Digby.
Satin embroidered with coloured silks, gilt and silver-gilt threads in stem, satin and long and short stitches, French knots, couched work and raised work. The ground is worked with couched silver-gilt thread to give a quilted effect.

Bequeathed by Miss E. F. J. Mackworth Dolben. T.95–1912 (Neg. No. 35814)

60. Coverlet, early 18th century

Part of a set of coverlet and pillows.
Linen quilted with yellow silk in back stitch and embroidered with red and yellow silks in long and short, stem and satin stitches with French knots and laid and couched work.

T.286–1927 (Neg. No. F.H.521)

61. Bed Hanging, c.1730 (detail)

Inscribed IT WAS BEGUN APRIL 22(?) 1729.
Two valances from the set are in the Department of Circulation, other single hangings are in the Royal Scottish Museum and the National Museum of Wales. The set is said to have been worked by Rachel Corbett, daughter of Vincent Corbett of Ynysmaengwyn.
Linen and cotton twill weave, embroidered with coloured wools in satin, stem and long and short stitches.

T.86–1928 (Neg. No. 62160)

62. Embroidered Carpet, second quarter 18th century

Canvas embroidered with coloured wools in tent stitch.

T.25–1952 (Neg. No. N.32)

63. Chair Seat, early 18th century

One of a set of twenty said to have been embroidered by Lady King (and her ladies), wife of Peter, Ist Baron King, Lord Chancellor, 1723–33. Canvas embroidered with coloured wools and silks in tent stitch.

Bequeathed by Dame Ethel Locke King. T.120m–1956 (Neg. No. Q.520)

64. Chair Seat, 1747

One of a pair, the other dated 1737.
Signed and dated PRUDENCE NISBITT 1747
Linen canvas embroidered with wool and silk in tent and cross stitches.

824–1904 (Neg. No. 59400)

65. Picture, c.1720

Initialled E.H. for Elizabeth Haines.
Woollen canvas embroidered with coloured silks in tent, satin and encroaching satin stitches.

Given by Mrs. E. G. Barrett. T.91–1934 (Neg. No. 70806)

66. Pole Screen Panel, first half 18th century

Canvas embroidered with coloured wools and silks in tent and cross stitches.

W.1–1928 (Neg. No. 59231)

67. Dress, c.1730 (detail of skirt)

Silk embroidered with coloured silks, gold and silver-gilt thread and metal purl in satin, stem, feather and long and short stitches with French knots, laid and couched and padded work.

Given by Miss Katherine Boyle. T.179–1959 (Neg. No. F.H. 1740)

68. Sleeved Waistcoat, 1745 (detail)

Made for the wedding of William Morshead of Carthuther, Cornwall, in 1745.
Satin embroidered with coloured silks and silver thread in long and short and satin stitches with couched work; sequins.

T.94–1931 (Neg. No. 66710)

69. Apron, early 18th century

Silk embroidered with coloured silks and silver and silver-gilt thread in long and short, satin, stem and outline stitches with French knots, laid and couched work and raised work.

597–1886 (Neg. No. 59394)

70. Chinoiserie Apron, 1717 (detail)

The apron bears several incomplete Biblical inscriptions and is signed and dated MARY TYKELL IN THE 14 YEAR OF HER AGE 1717.
Muslin embroidered with white cotton in satin, chain, stem and darning stitches with drawn fabric work in a variety of diaper designs.

1564–1904 (Neg. No. 33959)

71. Quilted Cover, early 18th century (detail)

Linen with Italian quilting in back and running stitches and with a variety of drawn fabric work fillings.

859–1897 (Neg. No. 27897)

72. Patchwork Hanging, second half 18th century (detail)

Patchwork with a shell or scale pattern made from printed cottons and linens of various dates and from different countries, including India.

Given by Major Harlow Turner. 242c–1908 (Neg. No. 68553)

73. Chairback, c.1780

Canvas embroidered with coloured wools in cross stitch.

W.36–1919 (Neg. No. 79078)

74. Firescreen Panel, 1792

Worked by Mary Ann Body in 1792.
Satin embroidered with coloured silks in long and short, satin and stem stitches.

Given by Miss F. M. Beach. T.108–1929 (Neg. No. 70274)

75. The Osterley Park House Bed, c.1776 (detail)

Designed by Robert Adam in 1776, recorded in the 1782 inventory.
Silk and velvet embroidered with coloured silks and chenille thread and coiled silver-gilt thread in stem, satin, long and short and split stitches with French knots and laid and couched work; trimmed with yellow fringe and tassels.

O.P.H. 29–1949 (Neg. No. M.2527)

76. Patchwork Quilt, c.1803 (detail)

The scene in the centre possibly represents one of two volunteer reviews held by George III on October 26th and 28th, 1803.
Made from printed cottons of 1790–1800 with additional embroidery with coloured silks in satin, long and short and chain stitches.

Given by Mrs. Gertrude S. Ferrabey. T.9–1962 (Neg. No. Y.1562)

77. Picture, late 18th century

Fame strewing flowers on Shakespeare's tomb.
Silk embroidered with coloured silks in long and short stitches. Details painted in water colour.

39–1874 (Neg. No. F.D.527)

78. Picture, 1825

Napoleon Buonaparte.
By Mary Linwood (1755–1845).
Canvas embroidered with coloured wools in long and short stitches.

1428–1874 (Neg. No. 55729)

79. Chair Back, c.1850

Linen canvas embroidered with coloured wools in silks in tent stitch.

Given by Mrs. L. E. Duck. T.5–1942 (Neg. No. 82672)

80. Chair Seat, c.1820

Linen canvas embroidered with coloured wools and silks in cross stitch.

Given by Brigadier General J. Dallas. T.104–1926 (Neg. No. 59392)

81. Picture, c.1845

The Prince of Wales and his dog.
Canvas embroidered with coloured wools in tent stitch.

Given by H.M. Queen Mary. T.141–1935 (Neg. No. M.2635)

82. Handscreen, c.1860

Morning.
The design adapted from Thorvaldsen's bas-relief.
Canvas embroidered with coloured silks and glass and metal beads in tent stitch.
Beadwork fringe.

Given by Brig.-Gen. J. Dallas. T.56–1925 (Neg. No. X.414)

83. Baby's Long Gown, second quarter 19th century (detail)

Fine cotton embroidered with cotton in raised satin, stem and buttonhole stitches and eyelet holes and with drawn fabric work and needlepoint fillings in a variety of designs.

Given by Miss E. Gibbard in accordance with the wishes of the late Miss Portal. T.96–1929 (Neg. No. 67175)

84. Smock, mid-19th century (detail)

A wedding smock from Lewes, Sussex.
Homespun white linen smocked and embroidered with linen thread in single and double feather stitches with French knots.

Given by Mr. Thomas Sutton. T.17–1918 (Neg. No. 46867)

85. Coverlet, c.1851 (detail)

In the centre a panel specially printed for applied work and two silhouette versions of the Greek Slave, copied from the sculpture by Hiram Powers shown at the Great Exhibition of 1851.
Applied work of printed cottons.

Given by the West Kent Federation of Women's Institutes T.86–1957 (Neg. No. S.356)

86. Coverlet, c.1876

Designed by William Morris and worked by Mrs. Catherine Holiday for Morris, Marshall, Faulkner & Co.
Linen embroidered with coloured silks in long and short stitches and couched work.

Circ.196–1961 (Neg. No. M.648)

87. Screen Panel, 1899

Embroidered by Miss E. D. B. Bradby (1861–1927).
Satin embroidered with coloured silks and silver-gilt thread in satin, long and short and outline stitches with French knots and laid and couched work.

Given by Mr. G. F. Bradby. T.270–1927 (Neg. No. F.G.441)

88. Cushion Cover, c.1900

Embroidered by Jessie R. Newbery of Glasgow School of Art.
Linen with linen applied work and embroidery with coloured silks in satin stitch and needle-weaving.

Given by Mr. Lang. T.69–1953 (Neg. No. K.837)

89. Curtain, c.1905 (detail)

One of a pair of curtains worked at the Royal School of Art Needlework for Fanhams Hall, Ware, Herts.
Cream silk damask embroidered with crewel wools and silks mainly in long and short stitches.

Given by the Westminster Bank Ltd. Circ.609–1964 (Neg. No. F.G.442)

90. Coverlet, early 20th century (detail)

Coverlet designed by Mrs. Arthur Newall of Fisherton-de-la-Mere, Wilts., and embroidered by her and Miss Kate Joliffe.
Home spun and hand woven linen embroidered with white linen in satin, brick, Hungarian, Vandyke, buttonhole, long and short and insertion stitches with French and bullion knots, eyelet holes, laid work and a variety of drawn fabric fillings. The edges are decorated with a knotted fringe.

Given by Mr. R. S. Newall. T.1–1924 (Neg. No. 53657)

91. Picture, c.1936–37

The Magic Garden.
Designed and worked by Mrs. Rebecca Crompton.
Worked in appliqué in patterned and coloured
silks and embroidered with coloured silks in
honeycomb stitch and French knots and couching.
Circ.10–1937 (Neg. No. 76404)

92. Picture, 1950

The Fabulous Cock.
By Mary Bryan.
Stamped velvet with applied work of various
materials, machine-embroidery in coloured silks
and cottons, beads and sequins.
Circ.196–1950 (Neg. No. J.961)

93. Picture, 1952

Madonna and Child.
Designed and worked by Margaret Traherne.
Muslin piqué, machine embroidered with green
sewing cotton.
Circ.133–1952 (Neg. No. L.1003)

...SLORVM:ETSVI MILITES:EQVI TANT:AD BOS HA...

2

3

4

6 (detail)

6

7

8

9

10

11

12

13

14

15

16

19

20

23

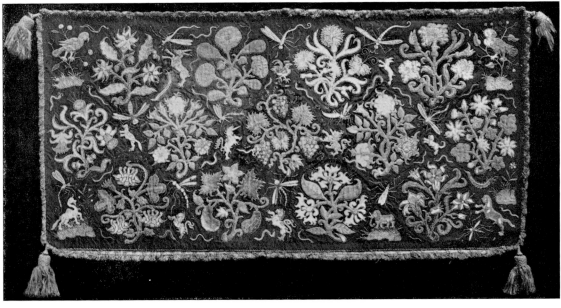

24

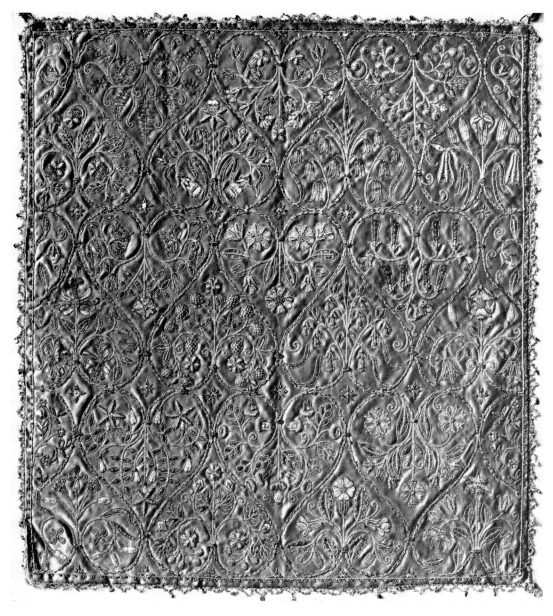

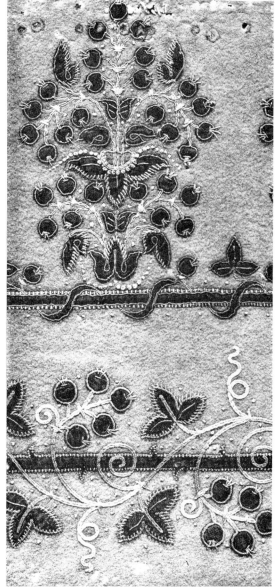

25

26

28a

28b

28c

29

30

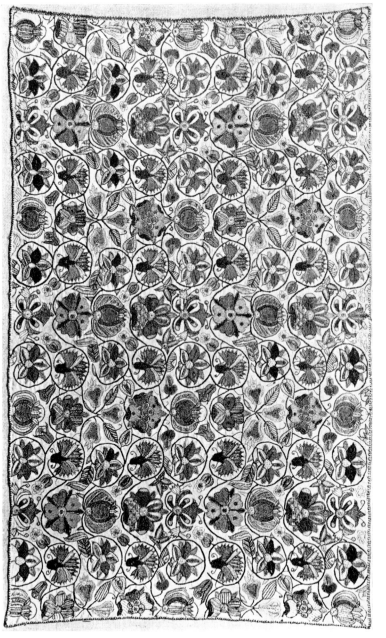

31

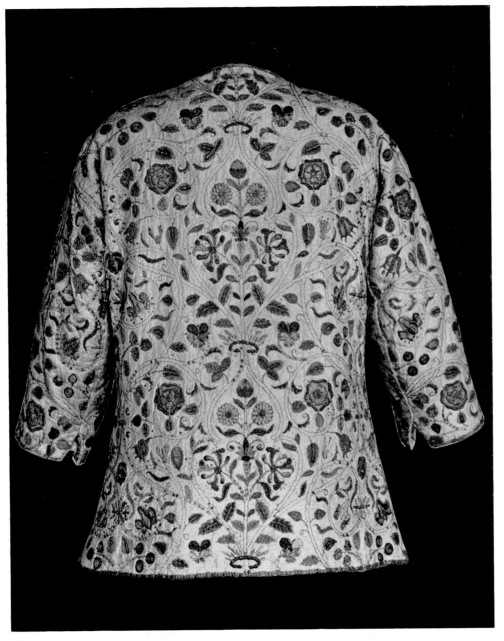

33

32

34

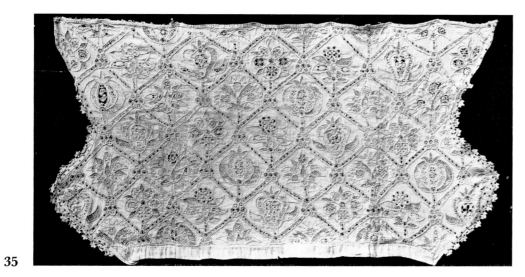

35

36

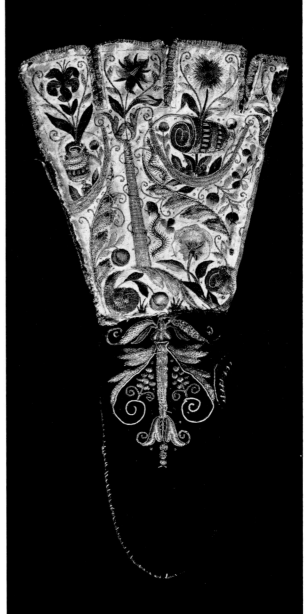

37

38

39

40

41

42

(detail)

43

44

45

46

47

49   50

51   52

53

55

57

58

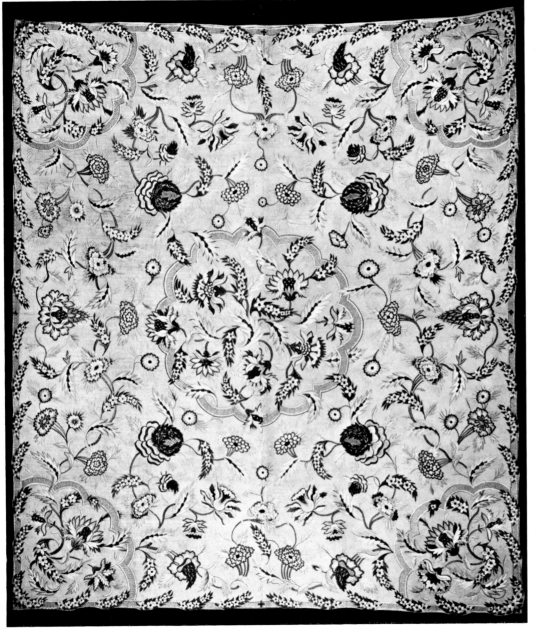

60   61

63

62

64

65

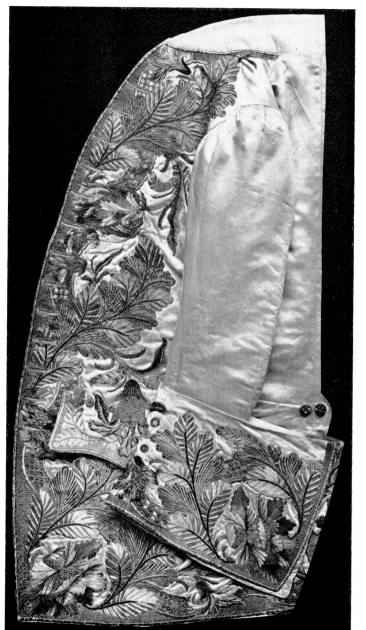

69

70

72

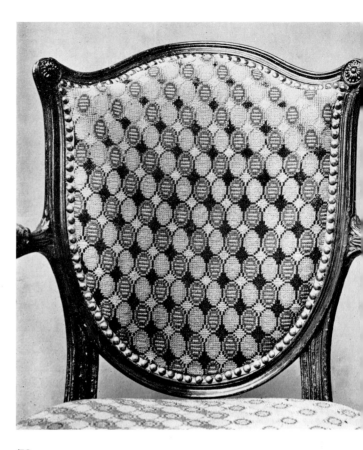

73

74

75

76

77

78

79

80

81

82

83

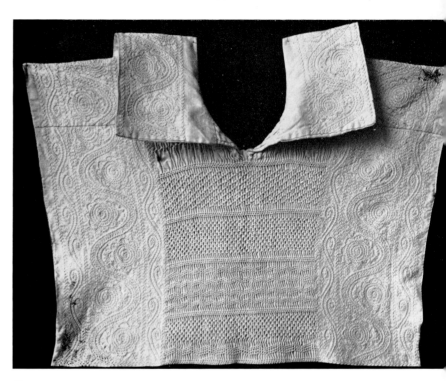

84

86

87

89

88

91

92

93